charles rennie MACKINTOSH

charles rennie
MACKINTOSH

FIONA AND ISLA HACKNEY

A QUANTUM BOOK

Published by Shooting Star Press, Inc.
230 Fifth Avenue, Suite 1212
New York, NY 10001
USA

ISBN 1-57335-505-4

This book was produced by
Quantum Books Ltd
6 Blundell Street
London N7 9BH

Creative Director: Peter Bridgewater
Art Director: Ian Hunt
Designer: Nicki Simmonds
Artwork: Danny McBride
Project Editor: Caroline Beattie
Editor: Patricia Bayer
Picture Researcher: Simon Green
Illustrator: Lorraine Harrison

Typeset in Great Britain by
Central Southern Typesetters, Eastbourne
Manufactured in Hong Kong by
Regent Publishing Services Limited
Printed in Singapore by
Star Standard Industries (Pte) Ltd

CONTENTS

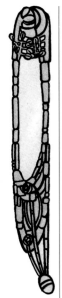

chapter one
ORIGINS

RIGHT Glasgow School of Art, west façade, detail of the Library windows. Mackintosh's dramatic use of iron and glass in the west wing anticipate later developments in twentieth-century Modernism.

OPPOSITE RIGHT Glasgow School of Art. View from the south-west, 1907–9. Considered to be Mackintosh's most important work, the west wing of the School drew heavily on nineteenth-century ideas while anticipating the functionalism of twentieth-century Modernism.

RIGHT Glasgow School of Art, decorative sculpture, north façade. The keystone carved in low relief over the entrance to the School is evidence of Art Nouveau-style detailing in Mackintosh's work.

Charles Rennie Mackintosh (1868–1928) is recognized today as one of the most remarkable architects working in Great Britain at the turn of the century. Mackintosh exploited what he called the 'spirit of the old' to produce something entirely new, thus effecting a distinctive synthesis of styles. His work drew heavily on 19th-century architectural practices, while anticipating the functionalism and clarity of 20th-century Modernism. This is demonstrated in his most important architectural work, the Glasgow School of Art (1897–9 and 1907–9), which, although considered a milestone in the Modern Movement, nonetheless contains elements of pure Art Nouveau.

Mackintosh was a designer of great versatility whose oeuvre included furniture, metalwork, stained glass, and carpet and fabric designs; he was also an accomplished painter, producing handsome watercolours. However, he always regarded himself primarily as an architect. His interest in other areas of design sprang from a desire for rigorous continuity in his buildings, whose interiors harmonized with their exteriors, down to the smallest decorative details. In this regard, Mackintosh was typical of a new breed of 'universal designer' associated with the Art Nouveau movement; among these talented, eclectic designers were the Belgian Henry Van de Velde (1863–1957) and Josef Hoffmann (1870–1956) of Vienna, who were happy to turn their creative minds to areas as diverse as buildings, glass, metalwork and even costumes.

Not surprisingly, it was on the Continent that Mackintosh was most readily appreciated as a major figure in the Art Nouveau movement. After his work was illustrated in the English journal, *The Studio,* in 1897 and an article on him appeared a year later in *Dekorative Kunst,* the German periodical, Mackintosh was invited to decorate a room at the Eighth Exhibition of the

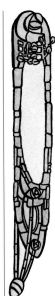

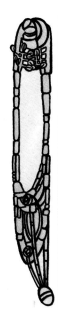

RIGHT Textile design (*c*1916–23). This rose and tear drop motif is just one among many distinctive designs for fabric produced by Mackintosh.

Vienna Secession in 1900. He was enthusiastically acclaimed by critics and public alike and thereafter contributed to exhibitions in a number of European cities. Indeed, Hoffmann's Palais Stoclet (1905–11) in Brussels – considered by most that architect's *chef-d'oeuvre,* and one of the finest examples of proto-Modernist architecture – displays a deeper understanding of Mackintosh's achievements than the work of any British architect of the time.

Despite his acclaim abroad, the majority of Mackintosh's architectural projects were built in and around his home town of Glasgow. During the second half of the 19th century Glasgow was a cosmopolitan city full of thriving commercial establishments, tea-shops and public houses. Buildings were commissioned by successful businessmen, the patrons of the new industrial age. These wealthy individuals used architecture to achieve cultural credibility both for themselves and their city. At the same time, the cultural life of the metropolis was enhanced by the art collections of such men as Archibald McLellan

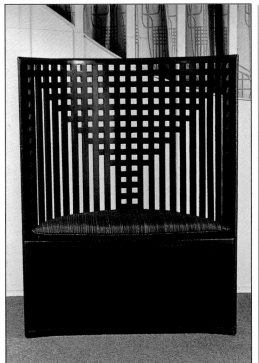

ABOVE Palais Stoclet, Brussels, 1905–11 by Josef Hoffman (1870–1956). A comparison between the architecture of Mackintosh and avant-garde Viennese designers working at the turn of the century reflect their shared aims and close association.

LEFT Chair from the Willow Tea Rooms (Glasgow). A distinctive and versatile designer, Mackintosh is particularly renowned for his designs for chairs. In this example he incorporated a symbolic willow tree pattern into the clear lines and geometric shapes of the chair back.

9

RIGHT The Sturrock domino mantel clock (1917). This clock is one of a group designed by Mackintosh in 1917, and is very similar to the one designed for WJ Bassett-Lowke. It was presented to Mary Newbery (the daughter of Fra Newbery) on the occasion of her wedding to Alec Sturrock in 1917. It was made in the Isle of Man by German prisoners of war.

OPPOSITE RIGHT Design for a clock. Mackintosh's style was carried into a wide range of designed items.

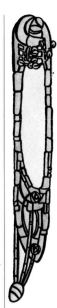

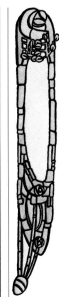

and Sir William Burrell. Culture was not confined to the privileged few, however: the Art Gallery and Museum at Kelvingrove opened to the public in 1902. The wealth enjoyed by some of Glasgow's citizens created a market, albeit a limited one, for adventurous art and design.

During the 1880s and 1890s Glasgow was the scene of a burst of creative activity, encompassing a broad spectrum of the visual arts. The painters known as the 'Glasgow Boys' met in the early 1880s in Ivy Macgregor's Bath Street studio. These artists, among them James Guthrie, EA Hornel, John Lavery and EA Walton, produced works of great originality, establishing a Glasgow school of Impressionist painting which was well respected both at home and abroad. The field of design and the applied arts was revitalized when, in 1885, Francis H Newbery, an Englishman of only 31 years of age, was appointed head of the Glasgow School of Art. He encouraged his pupils to develop their individuality and, under his enlightened guidance, a distinctive and extraordinary manner of painting and decorating evolved, which became known through-

out Europe as the 'Glasgow Style'. The main exponents of this idiosyncratic variation of Art Nouveau were Mackintosh, J Herbert MacNair (1868–1955) and the Macdonald sisters, Margaret (1864–1933) and Frances (1873–1921) – who became known as the 'Glasgow Four' – as well as Talwin Morris (1865–1911), Jessie Newbery (1864–1948) and George Walton (1867–1933). They shared a vocabulary of stylized, organically inspired motifs, particularly roses, foliage, butterflies and willowy human figures.

In order to assess the full measure of Mackintosh's achievement as an architect and designer, his work must be examined within the context of prevailing styles in Great Britain and Europe. Indeed, his unique vision derived from a wide range of influences, both historical and contemporary.

Between 1890 and 1910 a new generation of visionary architects emerged on both sides of the Atlantic, challenging the old guard and creating bold structures, some highly decorative and organic, others deceptively simple and rectilinear. Men such as Josef Hoffmann and

ABOVE The Robie house, Chicago, Frank Lloyd Wright, 1907–9. This house marks the climax of Wright's Prairie Style houses.

OPPOSITE LEFT Casa Batlló (detail of façade), Barcelona, 1905, Antonio Gaudí. Distinctive national styles were evolved by Mackintosh in Scotland, Antonio Gaudí in Spain, and Frank Lloyd Wright in the United States.

Otto Wagner in Austria, Victor Horta in Belgium and Hector Guimard in France, as well as the Spaniard Antonio Gaudí and American Frank Lloyd Wright, were all committed to developing new styles in their respective countries. These innovative quasi-nationalist tendencies were also seen in the work of Charles Rennie Mackintosh. Like Guimard, Hoffmann et al, he moved away from historicism and formulated a distinctive architectural vocabulary, which in turn was later to help shape the new 'International Style'.

Mackintosh's immediate roots in Great Britain were strong and far-reaching. In 1890 the British archictectural scene was very promising and was followed closely by the rest of Europe. In 1904–5 the architect Hermann Muthesius (1861–1927), former cultural attaché to the German embassy in London, produced his influential study, *Das Englische Haus*. Nine-teenth-century developments in architecture had tended towards a strident nationalism that emphasized the British condition and British history. This was largely due to the influence of the neo-Gothic architect, AWN Pugin (1812–52), whose theories fundamentally changed the course of British architecture. Pugin focused attention on the question of 'morality'; he be-lieved that architecture was only as good as the society that produced it. This resulted in the infusion of moral terms such as 'truthful expression' and 'honest structure' into archi-tectural thought and terminology. Pugin was a fervent Roman Catholic convert and medieva-list; his ideas spread rapidly due to the mid-19th-century enthusiasm for all things Gothic and the enormous influence of the Ecclesiologi-cal Society, founded by John Mason Neale and Benjamin Webb in 1839 as the Cambridge Camden Society, which encouraged the study of ecclesiastical architecture and the restoration of damaged churches. Pugin's ideas and forms were adapted to the requirements and techni-ques of Victorian society by two major architect members of the Ecclesiological Society, William Butterfield (1814–1900) and George Edmund Street (1824–81), as demonstrated, for example, by the former's All Saints, Margaret Street, London (1849).

By 1870, the heated debate between 'Gothic' and 'Classic' – the so-called 'battle of the styles' that had raged during the mid-19th century – subsided, to be replaced by a revival of the style of 'the brick architecture of Queen Anne and

LEFT The Red House, Kent, 1959–60, Philip Webb (1831–1915). This house designed for William Morris marked a return to a tradition of simple domestic building by Webb and his contemporaries in the Arts and Crafts Movement.

RIGHT An example of traditional Scottish vernacular architecture, *c*1600. Mackintosh likewise looked to traditional vernacular forms and detailing.

OPPOSITE RIGHT

Alexander 'Greek' Thomson, the leading architect of the 'Neo Grec', combined motifs from Greek, Roman and Italian sources to create a distinctive architectural style for the streets of Glasgow.

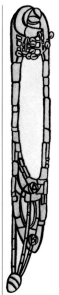

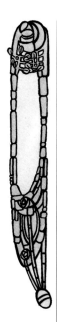

RIGHT Hill House, Helensburgh. In this building traditional Scottish features are clearly in evidence – plain harled walls, a corner stair tower and the uneven roof line.

the early Georges'. In effect this revivalism answered Pugin's call for an architecture that established continuity with the past while retaining a degree of flexibility and rationality. One of the champions of the Queen Anne style, JJ Stevenson, recommended for Scotland the adoption of the 'Scottish Baronial' style, with its appeal to a native tradition and its no-nonsense functionalism. These ideas were exploited in the works of Charles Rennie Mackintosh.

The importance of reviving old skills and techniques was promoted by William Morris, CR Ashbee and other figures of the Arts and Crafts Movement, whose philosophies emphasized (theoretically if not always actually) the quality of life and fraternity of the workmen. In 1877 Morris founded the Society for the Protection of Ancient Buildings, which disseminated knowledge of medieval building techniques and the 'behaviour' of materials. For people such as architect Philip Webb (1831–1915), a leading light of the society, the question of 'style' became irrelevant; he believed that a building, if constructed well and rationally in response to specific conditions and using native materials, would assume its own inherent form. A tradition of simple domestic building evolved, exemplified by Webb's Red House (1859–60), Bexleyheath, built for newlyweds William and Jane Morris, or the cheerful, cosy houses of CFA Voysey (1857–1941) and MH Baillie Scott (1865–1945). Voysey's house at Gartmell Fell, Windermere, for instance, demonstrates the new fashion for simple vernacular building with its plain white walls, low-pitched roof, overhanging eaves and long horizontal groupings of windows. This architecture, with its ruthless simplicity and its emphasis on craft and nature, had a considerable influence on Mackintosh. A strong belief in the crafts, in nature and in the symbolic power of architecture is revealed in a lecture he delivered in 1893, for which he relied heavily on the ideas of architect and educator WR Lethaby (1857–1931), a leading exponent of the Arts and Crafts Movement.

Mackintosh's architecture must be seen in relation both to general trends of architectural development and to native building traditions in Scotland. The persistence of feuds in the Middle Ages retarded the transition from defensive building to civic and domestic architectural work. Strong fortified towers, rectangular in plan and often with corner wings, lasted

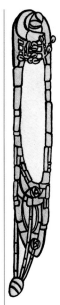

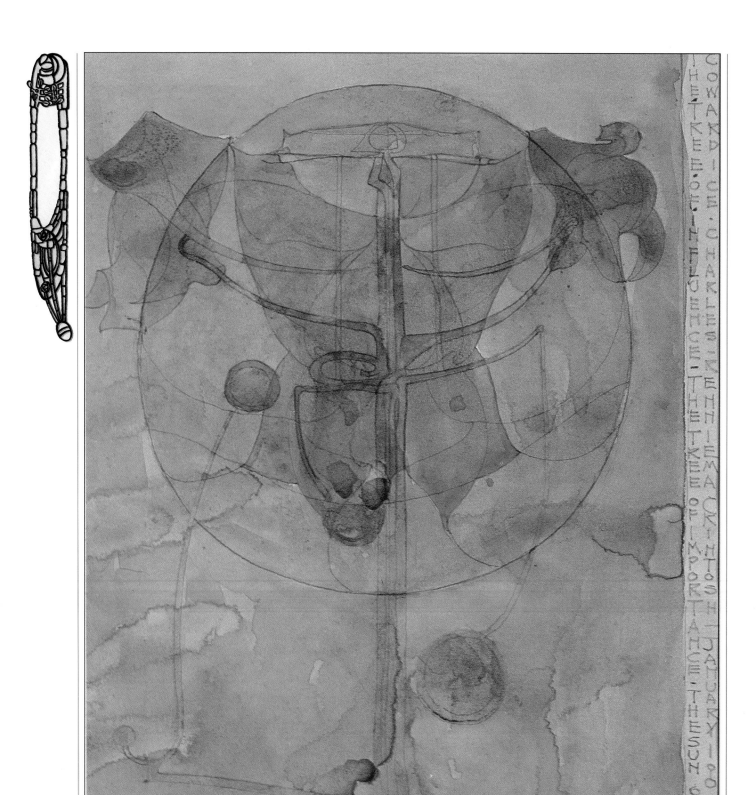

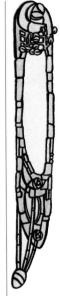

well into the 17th century. An increasing need for comfort and spaciousness led to the extending of upper stages and the development of ingenious devices such as massive corbels and enlarged angle turrets. Along with corbie-stepped gables and sturdy chimney stacks, these produced a picturesque and dramatic effect.

The typical Scottish burgher's house was a more homely and unpretentious dwelling. Generally conceived on a simple plan, it was made of rough-cast (harled) stone with few, irregularly placed windows; roofs were steeply pitched and gabled, while the lines of sweeping eaves were often interrupted by dormers lighting an attic. Angle turrets were used as rooms, rising through several storeys, occasionally enclosing a newelled staircase. Massive chimney stacks and gables gave a strong vertical emphasis. Typical examples are Lamb's House in Leith and Stenhouse in Edinburgh. The dour, uncompromising nature of these buildings is characteristic of the Scottish vernacular style, which allowed little room for comfort and refinement.

After the Reformation and the Union of Scotland and England, a great many changes took place. Renaissance Classicism became extremely popular in 18th-century Scotland: pediments, balusters and cornices appeared, while attempts were made at symmetrical planning. The new style was particularly associated with the work of William Adam (1689–1748) and his sons, Robert (1728–92) and James (1732–94). It was during this period that Edinburgh New Town was built, with its formal squares, crescents and regimented facades – in essence, the antithesis of the Scottish-style 'Old Town'. By the first quarter of the 19th century the so-called 'Greek Revival', spearheaded by such architects as William H Playfair (who designed the National Gallery of Scotland, 1850) and Thomas Hamilton (architect of the Royal High School, 1825–29), earned Edinburgh the epithet 'Athens of the North'. In Glasgow a modified style emerged – the neo-Grec, which combined motifs from Greek, Roman and Italian sources. The most influential figure in the neo-Grec style was Alexander 'Greek' Thomson (1817–75). His fresh and stimulating approach produced dignified terraces, extraordinary churches and fine city buildings characterized by a strange blend of Hellenic

ABOVE A contemporary photograph of Mackintosh's drawing room, showing his collection of Japanese-style flower arrangements.

OPPOSITE LEFT *Tree of Influence*, watercolour. Greater emphasis on organic imagery is evident in Mackintosh's work.

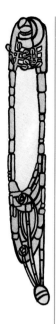

and Egyptian forms. Thomson created a distinctive local style that greatly influenced the street architecture of Glasgow.

The mid-19th century witnessed the emergence of the heterogeneous Scottish Baronial style and emphasis on the revival of Scotland's history and past glories, in part spurred by Sir Walter Scott and his 'Waverley' novels. Increased demand for architecture in the romantic manner led to self-conscious buildings adorned with crow-stepped gables, castellated parapets and Franco-Scottish turrets. With its air of fantasy, the royal residence of Balmoral – built on the site of a 15th-century castle and first occupied by Victoria and Albert in the 1850s – is a characteristic work of the Baronialists. Amid this theatricality a number of architects attempted to recapture the spirit of the vernacular, reviving traditional building methods: for example, Sir Robert Lorimer's cottages at Colinton, outside Edinburgh, and the buildings of James Maclaren and Dunn & Watson at Glenlyon, Perthshire,

which recall 17th-century Scottish architecture. However, it was Charles Rennie Mackintosh who fully exploited vernacular revivalism, working in a style close to that of the Maclaren circle but more distinctively Scottish in proportion and profile, as exemplified by his architectural projects around this time, Windyhill (1899–1901) and Hill House (1902–4).

At the same time, contemporary trends in art and design played a significant role in the formation of Mackintosh's style. He was not working in isolation; the Glasgow movement was a local symptom of a more widespread revolt against convention in all the arts. A major influence which led artists to free themselves from the past was the art and architecture of Japan, primarily known in Glasgow art circles through Japanese prints, which were widely available and immensely popular. Photographs of Mackintosh's Mains Street flat reveal that he owned Japanese artefacts and prints, and his exquisitely rendered flower drawings clearly demonstrate

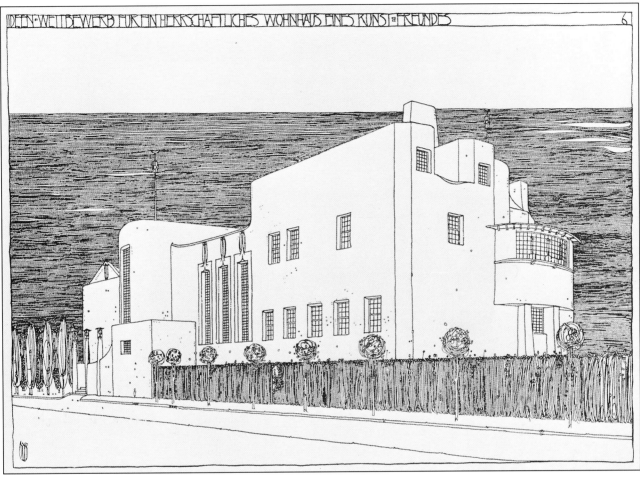

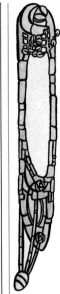

the influence of Japan. Dr Christopher Dresser's *Japan, its Architecture, Art and Art Manufacturers* was published in 1882, when Mackintosh was commencing his studies; this influential volume in part dealt with the traditional Japanese dwelling, which was built entirely of wood with internal divisions comprising opaque paper screens (thus enabling several rooms to be made into one). For Mackintosh, the Japanese house suggested exciting possibilities of freedom, spaciousness and flexibility – as well as a new aesthetic. He began to use openwork screens, balconies and a square post-and-lintel construction, elements which are evident in the interiors of Miss Cranston's Tea Rooms and the library of the Glasgow School of Art.

Since its inception in 1893, *The Studio* magazine was the chief vehicle for the dissemination of avant-garde design ideas. It was the only British magazine to give the Glasgow designers any support, and its wide distribution made the work of the Four available throughout the world. It

was also through the pages of *The Studio* that Mackintosh, MacNair and the Macdonald sisters became aware of the graphic work of Aubrey Beardsley (1872–98), which was to influence their own nascent style. Beardsley's position as art editor of John Lane's quarterly, *The Yellow Book*, and his 1894 illustrations for Oscar Wilde's *Salome* brought him rapid fame and notoriety – this just as the Glasgow Four were beginning to emerge.

Another potent stimulus in the evolution of the Glasgow Style was the Celtic Revival. The resurgence of the national spirit in Scotland was encouraged by Romilly Allen's researches into the origins of Celtic art and Partick Geddes' writings of the 1890s. Geddes' quarterly magazine, *Evergreen* – with its emphasis on nature, the seasons, birth, and death – formed a precise literary equivalent to the visual work of the Macdonald sisters, which in turn was to influence Mackintosh, future husband of Margaret Macdonald.

ABOVE Drawing for *Haus eines Kunstfreundes* (House of an Art Lover), view from the north-west, 1901. Although never built, Mackintosh's proposal won a special prize in the competition sponsored by the German magazine *Zeitschrift für Innendekoration* and helped spread his growing reputation abroad.

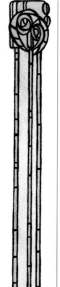

chapter two
THE EARLY YEARS

ABOVE Charles Rennie Mackintosh (1868–1928). A photograph which dates from around 1900–03.

OPPOSITE RIGHT Watercolour of Orvieto Cathedral. In 1891 Mackintosh was awarded a travelling scholarship which enabled him to study Italian architecture.

His childhood was a happy one, and he determined early in life to become an architect. With no artistic precedents in the family, it is a clue to his independent spirit that, at the age of 16, Mackintosh overcame parental opposition and joined the local architectural firm of John Hutchison; in the same year (1884), he enrolled as an evening student at the Glasgow School of Art.

Mackintosh's training was that of a typical Victorian architect in the 1880s. As an apprentice he would learn the practical and professional skills of architecture, earning by the fifth and final year of his training an acceptable wage of £25 per annum. At college he would be taught the rudiments of freehand and measured drawing, working either from plaster casts of Greek and Roman statues or from revered examples of local architecture.

An enthusiastic and conscientious student, Mackintosh was soon gaining acclaim with numerous prize-winning projects, attracting notice within the architectural profession as a name to be watched. Having completed his training and joined the firm of Honeyman and Keppie, Mackintosh entered and won the Alexander Thomson Travelling Scholarship. This financed an Italian tour in 1891 – he visited, among other places, Rome, Venice, Florence, Orvieto and Sicily – and set the seal on Mackintosh's professional status, giving him added confidence at the very outset of his career.

In spite of the success of Mackintosh's early projects, there is little suggestion in them of the individualism which was so soon to set Mackintosh apart. Completed under the supervision of the Art School or his office and carefully fulfilling the stipulated competition requirements, each project employed one or another of the revivalist styles of the time. Between 1890 and 1893 he designed a Greek public hall, a French Renaissance museum, a Classical chapter house

Today the exaggerated form of Charles Rennie Mackintosh's black-painted, high-backed chair of 1903 (which has been reproduced by Cassina of Milan) is instantly recognizable as his work. However, to fully appreciate the highly individualistic style of this versatile designer – some of whose creations have become icons of Modernism – the formative experiences of his training and early working life, his influences and associations, must be considered.

Mackintosh was born in Glasgow on 7 June, 1868, the second son of a family of 11 children.

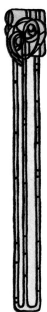

ORVIETO.

CRM
1891.

and a Gothic railway station. Clearly attempts to meet the jurors' approval, these projects left little room for anything new or challenging.

Thus these early, somewhat academic schemes seem to indicate Mackintosh's desire to assert himself within the architectural profession rather than to step outside it. Such determined professionalism is again evident in his readiness to lecture on current architectural issues. At the age of 22 Mackintosh delivered the first of three papers to an audience of eminent peers at the Glasgow Architectural Association. It is in these written statements that one gains a stronger sense of Mackintosh, his ideals and allegiances, and his ultimate independence of spirit.

In the first lecture, devoted to Scottish Baronial architecture, Mackintosh emphasized his belief in native Scottish traditions, extolling 'the architecture of our own country . . . as indigenous as our wild flowers, our family names, our customs or our political constitutions'. Yet, alluding to the recent work of Maclaren, Dunn and Watson, he promoted the possibilities of a new architecture linked with the past, but not bound by it. By believing in a 'valid' architecture, one appropriate to the land and society whence it came, Mackintosh declared his allegience to an ideology initiated by the architect AWN Pugin and John Ruskin (1819–1900), the influential writer who championed both the Gothic Revival and the Arts and Crafts Movement.

A lecture of 1893 reveals Mackintosh's debt to WR Lethaby, particulary that architect-designer's theories expressed in *Architecture, Mysticism and Myth*, a book published the previous year. Pleading with his fellow architects to abandon their self-conscious use of antiquarian detail, Mackintosh advised them to 'go straight to Nature'. His call to 'clothe modern ideas with modern dress', a bold condemnation of the type of eclecticism revealed in his own competition work, may have found favour among the more enlightened sections of his profession but was hardly guaranteed to please his audience of establishment architects. Such criticism of current architectural practice is evidence of an assertive and powerful individual. The sketches and diaries from his trip to Italy, the subject of yet another lecture, reveal Mackintosh's immense energy and afford glimpses of the wit and originality that were soon to come to the fore in his work.

Searching for a new, appropriate architecture,

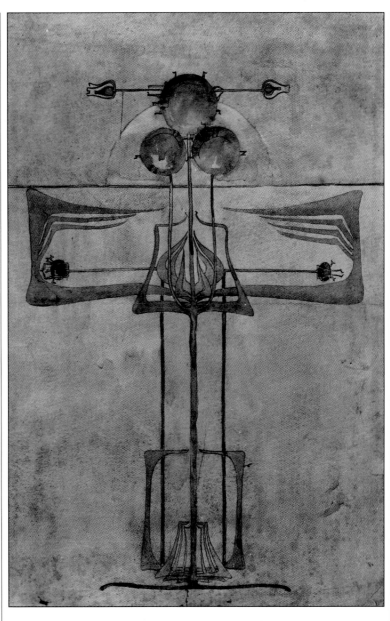

Mackintosh expanded his repertoire of organic and vernacular forms through sketches, watercolours and craftwork. From an early age he had been taught by his father, a keen gardener, to respect nature; its varieties of form, texture and colour soon proved an invaluable source of inspiration. Nor did he confine his attention to nature; the traditional forms, methods and materials of vernacular architecture proved equally stimulating. His childhood habit of sketching whenever he could, later continued in the company of his friend and colleague, Herbert MacNair, enabled Mackintosh to evolve a highly personal visual vocabulary which permeated

ABOVE Stylized plant form, watercolour. The elongated proportion and organic imagery which recur in Mackintosh's designs for chairs, posters and architecture were originally evolved through plant studies.

OPPOSITE LEFT Ill Omen, watercolour by Frances Macdonald, 1893.

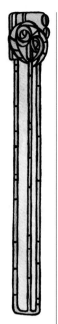

OPPOSITE RIGHT Japanese Witch Hazel. A watercolour study.

the rest of his work.

Together Mackintosh and MacNair developed a new graphic language. Discovering the emotive potential of the intricate linear patterns and coloured washes in his work, Mackintosh began to experiment with imagined rather than observed imagery. MacNair, also working for Honeyman and Keppie, was similarly involved in the search for new symbolic forms. The curiously disconcerting air to their work – with its undulating lines, animal and vegetable forms, and strong colours – is closer in spirit to Continental developments, eg, Symbolism and Art Nouveau, than to the practical, straightforward Arts and Crafts tradition of Great Britain. Mackintosh and MacNair, working independently of Art Nouveau, can even be said to have anticipated it somewhat with their early watercolours, which mark the beginnings of the Glasgow Style.

A thriving industrial city, Glasgow was enjoying a cultural revival by the 1890s, and the Glasgow School of Art, with Francis (known as Fra) Newbery as its director, was fast becoming one of the most influential art schools in Britian. It was here that Mackintosh and MacNair first met the Macdonald sisters, with whom they became closely linked, both professionally and personally. Margaret and Frances Macdonald, daughters of an English solicitor, had first settled in Scotland in the 1880s, enrolling at the Glasgow School of Art in 1891. The four students were introduced by Newbery, who noticed the remarkable similarity in their work and encouraged them to exhibit together. The innovative early work of 'The Four', as they were to be known, firmly established the Glasgow Style and their example was soon followed by several generations of Glasgow students.

The haunting quality of Frances Macdonald's *Ill Omen,* or *Girl In The East Wind,* of 1893 is typical of the early watercolours by The Four. A young girl is silhouetted against a dark blue, moonlit sky, her attenuated form and horizontal stream of fair hair echoed in the line of trees and flight of ravens behind her. The ghostly hues – yellow-greens and blues – applied in thin washes add to the mysterious, dramatic effect. Another example, *The Tree of Influence* (1895) by Mackintosh, reveals both similarities and differences in the work of The Four. With its motif of an elongated female form against a full moon, *The Tree of Influence* is comparable in style and imagery to *Ill Omen,* yet it is decidedly more

optimistic than Macdonald's work. Moving away from the eerie twilight world favoured by the sisters, Mackintosh places more emphasis on images of growth – root, stem, branch, bud and flower – all organic matter whose surging vertical lines are reflected in so much of his subsequent work.

Following their watercolour work, The Four collaborated on poster designs which proved to be highly original. In the early 1890s, when commercial advertising was still in its infancy, the hybrid forms portrayed by the Glasgow designers caused something of an outcry. One of their defenders was Gleeson White, editor of *The Studio,* who wrote:

> *. . . It must never be forgotten that the purpose of a poster is to attract notice, and the mildest eccentricity would not be out of place provided it aroused curiosity and so riveted the attention of passers-by. Mr Mackintosh's posters may be somewhat trying to the average person . . . But there is so much decorative method in his perversion of humanity that despite all the ridicule and abuse it has excited, it is possible to defend his treatment . . .*

Two designs from 1896, posters for the Glasgow Institute of Fine Arts and *The Scottish Musical Review,* are particularly impressive examples of The Four's controversial graphic style. Over 7 ft (2.10 m) high, these extraordinary posters – tall and narrow with distinctive decorative lettering and bold, stylized images – could not fail but attract attention; the subsequent public outrage only serves to highlight the innovative nature of such work.

In the Glasgow Institute poster, the Macdonald sisters and MacNair employed a shared vocabulary of stylized organic imagery and willowy human forms. Favourite motifs – lilies, thorny-stemmed roses and flying birds – are used while the strange bulb shape evident in so much of their work is repeated in the forms of the lilies, the cupped hands and the flowing hair of the figures. The *Musical Review* poster by Mackintosh is equally arresting. A sinister cloaked figure, her head silhouetted against a large halo, is flanked by doves and enshrined in an ornamental framework of lines. The sombre

JAPANESE
WITCH
HASEL
WALBERSWICK
1 9 1 5
C R M M
M M

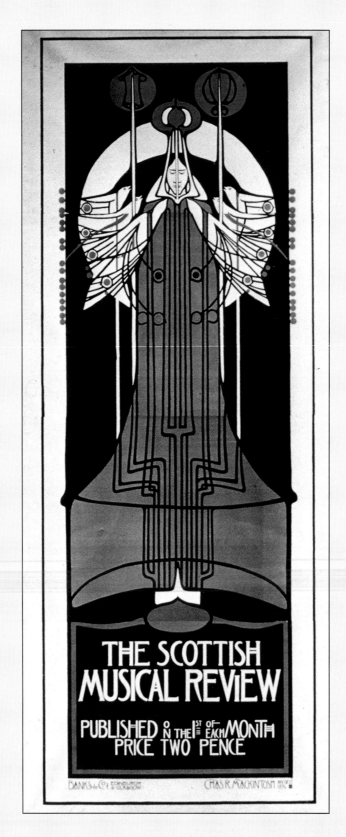

ABOVE Scottish Musical Review poster, 1896. Charles Rennie Mackintosh.

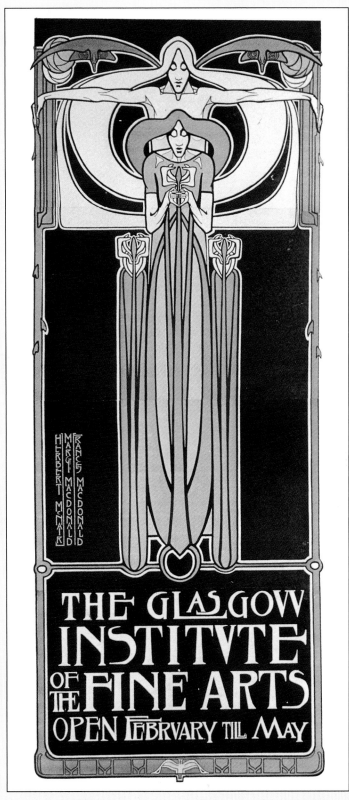

ABOVE Glasgow Institute Poster, *c*1896. Herbert MacNair and the
Macdonald sisters. 'The Four' collaborated to design some highly
original posters.

colour scheme of muted browns, blacks and rich blue is relieved by touches of emerald green in the birds' wings and tail feathers and in the circular emblems at the top of the composition. A severe abstracted image, it retains the highly decorative quality of so many Mackintosh designs. An interesting diversion from architecture, poster design soon proved a useful experience for Mackintosh, *vis-à-vis* subsequent mural commissions and wall-stencilling work.

The personal style formulated by The Four in their watercolours and poster designs was repeatedly used in an increasingly versatile range of decorative work. Their eerie, unsettling images – of melancholy human figures, bony hands outstretched and hair flowing, intertwined with plant stems, buds and roots – appear on mirror frames, clock faces and candlesticks alike. The contorted and convoluted linear patterns of their designs adapted well to other forms of craftwork they did – gesso panels, repoussé metalwork, stained glass and embroidered panels among them.

In 1895 Mackintosh rented a small studio where he worked on decorative commissions in his spare time. The Macdonald sisters had opened a studio the previous year on graduating from the Art School and MacNair, having completed his articles at Honeyman and Keppie, set up on his own, specializing in craftwork and furniture design. Apart from a contract received by Mackintosh to design furniture for Messrs Guthrie & Wells, Glasgow cabinetmakers, much of The Four's work at this stage was commissioned by friends or intended for exhibition. Before long their studios became the gathering place for Glasgow's artistic community. John Buchan, James Pryde, Jessie M King, Talwin Morris and countless others visited The Four, as did many young artists and designers, students from the Art School who were soon perpetuating the Glasgow Style.

ABOVE Design for the Diploma of the Glasgow School of Art. Mackintosh employed the symmetrically arranged female figures, curvilinear patterns of curling hair and stylized plant forms which came to typify work by the Four.

OPPOSITE LEFT *Danae or The Tower of Brass*, Edward Burne-Jones. A new type of female beauty with pallid features, heavy hair and long, flowing robes was created by Pre-Raphaelite painters.

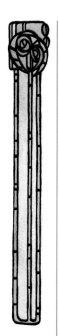

ABOVE Japanese prints which were imported into Europe in vast quantities during the period had a far-reaching effect on art and design in the West.

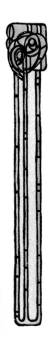

ABOVE Salome The Eyes of Herod, Aubrey Beardsley. The effective
use of black and white combined with plain areas contrasted
against areas of rich ornament reveal the influence of Japanese
prints.

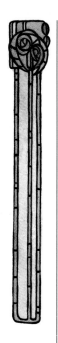

News of The Four's distinctive style had spread beyond Scotland by 1896, the year that they were asked to exhibit with the Arts and Crafts Exhibition Society in London. Unfortunately, the work they chose to show – mainly posters, watercolours and beaten metalwork – failed to win them the support of their English contemporaries, who associated their 'Spook School' style with the much-derided 'squirms' of Continental Art Nouveau. The ethereal mood of the Glasgow work also linked it with the current trend for Aestheticism and its spokesman Oscar Wilde, which did not help endear it to the hard-core supporters of the Arts and Crafts Movement in Britain.

One of the few Englishmen to respond favourably to the Glasgow designers' contribution was *The Studio*'s Gleeson White, who promptly decided to pay them a visit. Expecting to find four languid 'Aesthetes', White was surprised to discover 'two laughing comely girls, scarce out of their teens' and a pair of serious-minded architects. *The Studio* was to prove crucial to Mackintosh and his colleagues. A well-illustrated article on their work appeared in the July issue of 1897, followed by another in September of the same year. Subsequent articles in foreign journals meant that within a very short space of time Glasgow became the focus of attention for many in the art world.

As the debate surrounding The Four grew, their peculiar style and its possible origins became the object of increased speculation. The assumption that Egyptian art must be a major influence was soon dispelled in a conversation with Gleeson White. Other more likely influences of Japanese art, the Pre-Raphaelites, and above all, nature, evident in the prints and flowers with which The Four chose to decorate their studios, seem to have gone unnoticed by White. Contemporaries like Gustav Klimt in Vienna, the Norwegian artist Edvard Munch and the Dutchman Jan Toorop were closer in spirit to the Glasgow Four than any of their British counterparts, with the exception of Aubrey Beardsley. In the premier issue of *The Studio* in 1893, White had printed an influential article on Beardsley and reproduced Jan Toorop's memorable painting, *The Three Brides* (1893). The impact of each was clearly evident in the distinctive style of The Four.

The curvilinear patterns, symmetrical arrangement and spiritual content of Toorop's painting were immediately echoed in The Four's subsequent work. Pairs of female figures, seen in profile with their long hair curling in tendrils around them, occur again and again in the Glasgow designs, as do the repeated rhythms of stylized plant life, lilies and roses used by Toorop. The vague, disquieting quality common to both found its literary equivalent in *Evergreen*, which featured in the melancholy poems and prose of Scotland's Celtic Revival. But whereas Toorop was indebted to his Indo-Germanic descent, The Four were influenced by Scotland's Celtic past, the convoluted patterns of plants and hair recurring in their designs recalling the intricate strapwork and grotesqueries of Celtic imagery. Aubrey Beardsley's illustrations, with their carefully orchestrated balance of black and white, and of plain areas and areas of concentrated detail, reveal the influence of Japanese prints. The Four's oeuvre, in which the figures are reduced to decorative motifs and sweeping rhythms, indicates their familiarity with Beardsley and his Japanese sources.

The successful business partnership of The Four was soon to come to an end, however. By 1899 MacNair and Frances Macdonald were married and had settled in Merseyside, where MacNair had been appointed Instructor in Decorative Design at Liverpool University. Working on the first of his major architectural projects, the new Glasgow School of Art, Mackintosh still found time to continue with his decorative commissions. Margaret, the elder of the two sisters, collaborated with him, designing beaten metal panels for his furniture. Their friendship blossomed and by 1900 they, too, were married – a fitting conclusion to the story of The Four.

ABOVE *The Opera of the Sea*, gesso panel by Margaret Macdonald.
The decorative motifs and sweeping rhythms resemble devices
employed by Beardsley and his Japanese sources.

chapter three
THE ARCHITECTURAL PROJECTS

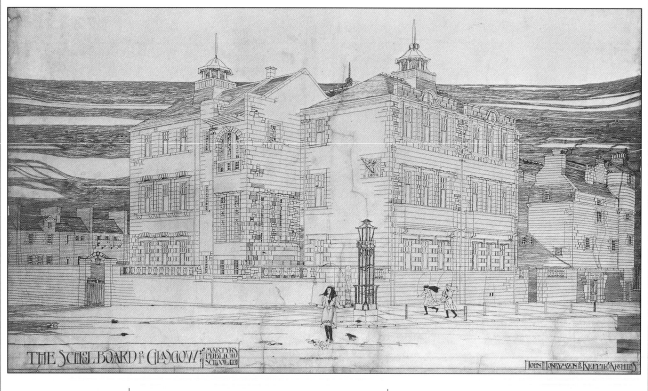

ABOVE Martyrs' Public School, perspective, 1895. While working for the firm of Honeyman and Keppie, Mackintosh developed an impressively bold yet refined style of line drawing.

It was in the field of architecture that Charles Rennie Mackintosh made his most significant contributions. During a period of intense activity from 1896 to 1906, he established himself as an architect of importance – indeed, a major influence on the architecture of the 20th century. Buildings such as the Glasgow School of Art and Hill House demonstrate that Mackintosh had developed a highly individual, even idiosyncratic style, characteristic of his own inventive and original temperament. However, these buildings were consciously rooted in Scottish traditions of architecture reaching back to the 17th and 18th centuries; for Mackintosh, it was of the greatest importance to evolve a vocabulary which maintained a continuity with the past while retaining a freedom of invention.

The stylistic origins of Mackintosh's major works may be seen in certain early architectural projects undertaken by Honeyman and Keppie, the firm with which he was closely associated. Three buildings are of particular interest: the *Glasgow Herald* building, Queen Margaret's Medical College and the Martyrs' Public School. The *Glasgow Herald* building, designed in 1893–94, is an ordinary Queen Anne, Scottish Baronial Victorian structure in all but the proportions and fenestrations of its Mitchell Street façade and, most importantly, the nature and appearance of its tower. These features are strongly identified with Mackintosh, as are the series of vertical windows arranged in the tower and the use of tall pilasters at the corners of the building, which recall the campanile at Siena,

LEFT The Glasgow Herald Building (detail). Although no longer home to this newspaper, the building is still in existence. The corner tower is a particularly distinctive feature which reveals Mackintosh's contribution to the design.

THE "HERALD" BUIL
MITCHELL St GL
OW. JOHN HONEYMAN AND K...

SCHOOL BOARD of GLASGOW. SCOTLAND STREET PVBLIC SCHOOL.

C.R.MACKINTOSH ARCH.
HONEYMAN KEPPIE & MACK.
140 BATH STREET GLASG.

which Mackintosh had praised during his Italian tour. The manner in which the coping to the parapet is swept up at an angle is another typical Mackintosh feature, while the ogee roof with its heavy weather-vane was a favourite feature and also appears in both the Medical College and the Martyrs' School.

The design for Queen Margaret's Medical College was completed in 1894. The building has since been incorporated into the Glasgow headquarters of the BBC and is best seen in a perspective drawn by Mackintosh (published in *The British Architect*, 10 January, 1896). The unique style of the drawing is characteristic of Mackintosh's work, whereby architectural and natural elements were carefully integrated. Although the authorship of the building was accredited to John Keppie, it is clear that Mackintosh played a considerable part in establishing the scheme. It consists of a very simple plan, the main rooms spiralling around a central vestibule which rises through two floors. The external forms and placement of windows directly reflect the internal spaces.

Mackintosh again drafted a beautiful perspective for the last building in this group, the Martyrs' Public School, designed *c*1895. This building has many features in common with the Medical College, among them the three tall staircase windows, relieving arches and corbelled sills. However, it is rather larger and the plan reveals

ABOVE Scotland Street School (north elevation). Perspective by WS Moyes, 1905. The separate entrances for each sex at the base of two projecting staircase towers answered the needs of the co-educational schooling system. The almost continuous vertical glazing confirm the precocious modernity of Mackintosh's work and anticipate developments abroad.

LEFT Scotland Street School. The south façade's repetitive fenestration is enlivened with a controlled use of Mackintosh's characteristic ornament.

OPPOSITE The Daily Record building, watercolour design by CR Mackintosh.

41

RIGHT Glasgow School of Art, 1897–9, detail of north façade. The distinctive metal plates on the entrance railings were inspired by Japanese heraldic shields.

RIGHT Glasgow School of Art, 1907–9. Detail of the Library windows.

a regulated symmetry due to the separation of the sexes traditional in Scottish schools. A new feature is a small section of roof which projects some 3 ft (90 cm) from the face of the wall and is supported by brackets – thus anticipating the eaves of the Glasgow School of Art. A novel visual effect is created by emphasizing the physical, constructional elements of the building rather than superimposing extra decorative elements. This treatment is continued in the interior of the building and is particularly evident in the jointing of the timber trusses in the main hall roof. These last elements were pure Mackintosh: features with a strong traditional bias were moulded into a form more in keeping with the architecture of his own country. These ideas were to be more fully developed in the Glasgow School of Art.

It is instructive to examine the commissions which ran concurrently with the evolution of the School of Art. The Queen's Cross Church was built in 1897–99, immediately after Mackintosh had finished his initial drawings for

LEFT The Glasgow Herald Building. Perspective by CR Mackintosh, *c*1893. An architectural project undertaken by the firm of Honeyman and Keppie, where Mackintosh worked for a time.

RIGHT Glasgow School of Art. A view of the north façade showing the main entrance.

BELOW Glasgow School of Art. A detail showing the unusual but decorative window brackets, which also serve as rests for window cleaners' equipment.

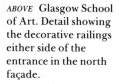

ABOVE Glasgow School of Art. Detail showing the decorative railings either side of the entrance in the north façade.

LEFT Glasgow School of Art. The west façade entrance which leads into the library wing.

ABOVE Glasgow School of Art, west elevation, 1897–9. Many of the forms which recur throughout Mackintosh's work are in evidence here.

OPPOSITE Glasgow School of Art. View of the main staircase from ground level and the porter's lodge.

the School of Art. The church is most notable for its traditional handling and modern detailing. The interior reveals exposed steel tie beams, rivets and plates – in effect, a medieval roof made of modern materials. Structural members are utilized in a decorative manner while the pulpit is decorated with carved ornament based on the floral motifs of the Glasgow Four. (In 1977 the former church became the international headquarters of the Charles Rennie Mackintosh Society and the focus of its activities, lectures and exhibitions.)

In 1901, the year of Glasgow's great International Exhibition, the building for the publishing house of the *Daily Record* was completed (the only remaining project drawing is a large perspective in the Glasgow University Collection). A large structure on Renfield Lane, near Glasgow Central Station, it is now used as a warehouse. The site was awkward and presented elevational problems, as it was enclosed on three sides by a narrow street and was consequently very dark. Mackintosh evolved the idea of using white glazed brick up to the fourth storey; this was relieved by occasional projecting bricks which emphasized the upward movement – a highly successful, sculpturesque treatment. In 1904 Mackintosh became an official partner in the firm of Honeyman and Keppie, and began to work on a new Glasgow school in Scotland Street. Its plan was symmetrical in pattern, clear and economical (this may have been due to the limited budget); indeed, all elements of the plan were clearly expressed in the building's form. Any external decoration was concentrated around doors and windows. Again, the architect linked past traditions with new interpretations.

The building for the Glasgow School of Art led to the beginning of Mackintosh's dramatic rise in European stature. The new structure was the result of a competition organized in 1895 by the governors. Francis Newbery's demand for extremely spacious classrooms – combined with a limited budget of £14,000 – made the task

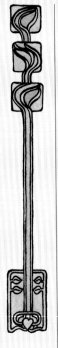

LEFT The eastern elevation of the Glasgow School of Art.

BELOW Glasgow School of Art. Studio in use as a general design room. The beam construction is of particular interest. The large window is south-facing, and a door in the left-hand corner gives access to a conservatory cantilevered out over the south façade.

ABOVE Glasgow School of Art. The Museum. The timber truss
work, exposed brackets and rafters reveal Mackintosh's debt to
Japanese architectural devices.

impossible. Eventually a two-stage design was decided upon, the existing money being used for the initial phase. In 1897 it was announced that the successful firm was Honeyman and Keppie, with Mackintosh's design. This immediately caused a furore; the scheme was accused of being too 'art nouveau' and it was widely known that Newbery was Mackintosh's friend and patron. However, the building went ahead; it contains the germ of Mackintosh's genius and development over the next 13 years. It is significant that the design itself was not final, but rather an indicator of the architect's intention, it was always open to alteration and improvement, in much the same way that an artist works on a sculpture, allowing the creation to take shape in his or her hands.

The design of the School of Art was amazing; nothing like it had been seen before, for there were no recognizable historical trappings such as cornices, columns, pediments or corbiestepped gables. Instead the building was uncompromisingly plain with its sweeping horizontal lines and vast 18-foot (5.40-m) windows relieved only by extraordinary decorative metal brackets. The plan was largely determined by the character of the site, which was a long, narrow rectangle bounded by Renfrew Street, Scott Street to the west and Dalhousie Street to the east. The principal access was on the north side, entering the ground floor at a fairly high level, a steep slope leading to the southern elevation. The west end of the basement was designed for clay modelling, sculptors' studios and the lecture theatre; the painters' studios were located on the north side to receive the constant northern light. The building, even today, exists very much as Mackintosh visualized it. His original plan was specially conceived in order to allow maximum flexibility – for instance, there are movable partitions between the studios, rather than solid walls, and the use of mezzanine floors compensates for the use of space in the principal rooms – the first floor ceilings reach a height of 26 feet (7.80 m). The materials used were solid masonry and brickwork, and the major spans were of steel lattice girders or castiron beams, encased in cement or metal laths.

The north façade, built between 1897–99 and 1907–9, demonstrates how Mackintosh subverted a symmetrical building by placing the main doorway asymmetrically. It is given emphasis by reducing the window openings to a

LEFT Glasgow School of Art. The Library. The room, which is still used as a library, contains tables, chairs, magazine racks and lights designed by Mackintosh. The gallery is set back 3ft (1m) from the main pillars on beams and the space in between filled with carved and decoratively coloured balusters.

51

RIGHT Glasgow School
of Art. The Director's
Office. One of the
earliest of Mackintosh's
'white' interiors, the
room is panelled to a
height of 8ft (2.43m)
and has a fine fireplace
with a wide mantel.

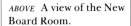

minimum and permitting a certain amount of decoration in and around the doorway itself, such as the modelled architrave and large keystone with its characteristic Mackintosh ornamentation. The entrance is further highlighted by the large semicircular headed French window on the first floor, which lights the principal's office, and its projecting metalwork balcony; above, an unbroken mass of masonry comprises the high parapet of a second balcony serving the principal's studio. To the left of this entrance 'unit', a tower – topped with a decorative wrought-iron motif of a bird and tree – houses the principal's staircase and, on the ground floor, the enquiry office.

The north façade is especially noted for Mackintosh's highly original use of wrought-iron decoration; this medium is used throughout the school to portray motifs which originated in the craftwork of The Four. Of particular significance is the important contribution made by Mackintosh in his creative use of Japanese models. The remarkable metal plates on the entrance railings are taken from Japanese 'mon', or heraldic shields – the specific sources have been found illustrated in the books on Japanese art in the School of Art Library. The projecting iron brackets to the studio windows fulfil a dual role; as decoration they relieve the severity of the façade, and as a support for window cleaner's planks they perform a very necessary function.

ABOVE A view of the New Board Room.

LEFT Glasgow School of Art. The New Board Room. Designed by Mackintosh to replace his original board room on the first floor (vacated to provide more studio space), the room's neo-Classical pilasters and traditional panelling indicate its serious function in a somewhat irrelevant way.

ABOVE Hill House, Helensburgh (1902–3). North view showing Mackintosh's use of a steeply pitched roof, dormer windows and irregular fenestration, features common to Scottish vernacular architecture. To the right of the door the main staircase is projected in a semi-circular curve setting it apart from the rest of the house.

Mackintosh's dramatic redesign of the west façade in 1906-7 produced one of his most daring and innovative compositions. Spectacular horizontal and vertical rhythms of glass and metal are juxtaposed against large plain areas of masonry in a highly original and uncompromising manner. Three massive windows, each reaching a height of 25 ft (7.50 m), provide the library with ample light. These windows are flanked on either side by linked mouldings, originally intended for carving. This would have introduced an element of figurative sculpture, emphasizing the library, while relieving the abstract nature of the façade. The windows of the adjoining south elevation are subtly incised to emphasize the high relief of the west façade. The entrance on this front is the building's most elaborate doorway, it was also intended to contain carved figures which remain unexecuted. The whole composition is brought to a conclusion by the three small horizontal windows and the triangular gable of solid masonry at the top of the building.

The wall of the east front rises to a height of 80 ft (24 m) or more. The northern section, an uncompromising sheet of masonry, is relieved only by the tiny projecting shelf at parapet level (the two lower windows are later additions). Mackintosh's drawing reveals that trees were originally intended to relieve the severity of the east front – an example of the architect's concern to unite his building with its environment. The southern section consists of an even surface of solid masonry and a number of symmetrically placed windows, a slightly projecting polygonal oriel separating the two. The overall appearance is of something entirely new and fresh. The south façade presents a complete contrast to the north: its windows are few and small, and it cannot be seen completely from any position at ground level. Mackintosh was aware of this and managed to convey an impression of immense size by his arrangement of the many small elements and irregular outline.

The interior of the buildng reveals the remarkable versatility of the designer. On entering

the main hallway the most striking feature is the staircase, with its open balustrading and interplay of light and shade, which motion one upward from the dark of the interior hall. The simple vertical emphasis of the high balustrade, with its square posts and caps, recalls the work of CFA Voysey and traditional Japanese interiors. The most important rooms in the building are, of course, the studios – they are airy and spacious, measuring 17 ft (5.10 m) from floor to ceiling on the ground floor, and 26 ft (7.80 m) on the first. The enormous glass windows and roof lights make ample provision for the plentiful yet diffuse light required by painters. An additional feature is the so-called 'hen run', a narrow glazed walkway, carried on iron brackets like a shelf, which provides magnificent views over the city while acting as a utilitarian connecting passage.

The library is one of the most significant interiors of the early 20th century. Mackintosh made great play of the aesthetic possibilities of heavy timber construction; the tall, square pillars of stained pine, which support the coffered ceiling, and the post-and-lintel construction of the gallery are clearly revealed. Solid panels are carved to produce an abstract pattern effect. The furniture – tables, chairs, magazine racks – were all designed by the architect. Of particular interest is the manner in which Mackintosh organized the lighting to provide an atmosphere conducive to study. He designed special light fittings which, with their box-like shades, directed light downwards to serve the desks, while the upper part of the room was left in shadow. The dark appearance of the library is actually deceptive, for it is well lit by the tall west windows. In the library Mackintosh moves away from the forms of 'art nouveau' towards an emphasis on structural concerns and problems of spatial organization.

The Director's office is one of Mackintosh's first 'white' rooms. The panelled fireplace, built-in cupboards, small leaded-glass panels and stair screen are all characteristic of an interior style which he developed in his domestic com-

ABOVE Hill House, Helensburgh (1902–3) Detail of the south façade showing the circular staircase tower, a feature traditionally employed in Scottish architecture.

missions. A very different emphasis was given to the new Board Room, the only major example of neo-Classical work executed by Mackintosh at the turn of the century. It presents a far more conventional appearance, although idiosyncratic notes, such as the highly inventive pilasters, betray the hand of the architect. Every detail of the School of Art reveals the careful attention of Mackintosh: it is a fascinating testament to his achievement. In addition to fulfilling its purpose admirably (it is still used as an art school today), the building is both a highly personal statement, as well as Mackintosh's most important contribution to modern architecture.

By the end of the 19th century British domestic archtecture had achieved an extremely high reputation both at home and abroad. In 1899 Mackintosh received his first independent commission, from the prominent businessman and art collector William Davidson, for Windyhill, his family house at Kilmacolm. The architect's other major domestic commission was from WW Blackie, the publisher, for his Hill House, near Helensburgh (1902–3). Both buildings combine elements of the traditional Scottish idiom with a treatment which was entirely new. By way of simple massing, the careful arrangement of shapes and the positioning of openings in the harled walls, Mackintosh transformed simple vernacular dwellings into milestones of modern architecture – this is particularly true of Hill House. There were many similarities between Hill House and Windyhill; for instance,

both were located on open, hillside sites. This reflects Mackintosh's preoccupations with landscape and integrating architecture with its surrounding environment. The architect paid particular attention to the garden at Hill House, laying it out with great care so that it appears to be a part of the natural landscape. This is reflected in the south front of the building, with its friendly and informal air, its overhanging eaves and projecting gable. The west front, which Hill House is first approached, is very different in character. It is far more imposing – the gabled wall is plain, apart from three small slit windows, and the sturdy chimney form produces a highly sculptural effect.

Central to Mackintosh's architectural philosophy was the belief that a building should fulfil the purpose for which it was designed. Contrary to general practice of the time, Mackintosh would not prepare any designs for the elevations of a house until the internal arrangements had been submitted and approved. The plans of a building are of primary importance to its function, and this took precedence over any formal considerations, such as symmetry. Mackintosh believed that a house should evolve as an organic whole, plan and elevation being fully integrated in the architect's concept of the building. The apparently random positioning of windows in an elevation reflects not only the priority of internal layout over external appearance, but is also part of an abstract composition, which results in a perfectly balanced composition of solid and void.

ABOVE Hill House, Helensburgh (1902–3), viewed from the southeast.

OPPOSITE LEFT Hill House, Helensburgh (1902–3). The main entrance approached from the west with views over the Firth of Clyde beyond.

59

chapter four

THE INTERIOR PROJECTS

ABOVE The Drawing Room, Southpark Avenue (reconstructed in the Hunterian Art Gallery).

OPPOSITE RIGHT The Entrance Hall, Southpark Avenue (reconstructed in the Mackintosh House, Hunterian Art Gallery, Glasgow). The muted colours employed by Mackintosh in the hall and dining room were offset by coloured glass and decorative metalwork.

Charles Rennie Mackintosh's interiors – harmoniously conceived and finished down to the last detail – are a striking example of the architect's unique vision. As a designer Mackintosh strove to create interiors wherein the architectural and decorative elements were totally integrated. His skilful manipulation of interior spaces – including colour, light, texture and furnishings – gave added meaning to some of the ideas implicit in his architectural work.

Mackintosh's approach to interior design is best exemplified by the account written by his client, Walter Blackie, of the evolution of the Hill House project. He recalled how Mackintosh insisted on spending time with the Blackie family to assess their 'life-style' and how it was only when agreement was reached on internal arrangements that Mackintosh proceeded to design the exterior elevations. The German art critic Hermann Muthesius, writing of The Four's work, had similarly noted their concern with, 'the room as work of art, as a unified organic whole, embracing colour, form and atmosphere' and how, 'starting from this notion they develop not only the room but the whole house, the sole purpose of the exterior of which is to enclose the rooms'.

Unfortunately, the opportunity to design both the exterior and interior of buildings did not arise as often as Mackintosh would have liked. Much of his interior work consisted of remodelling existing apartments. In the domestic field Hill House and its predecessor, Windy-

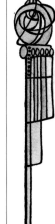

LEFT The Studio-Drawing Room, Southpark Avenue (reconstructed in the Hunterian Art Gallery). One section of the L-shaped drawing room was designed as a studio.

hill, were two rare examples whose commissions enabled him to expound his ideas on the integration of architecture, decoration and furniture. In both cases Mackintosh was fortunate to secure the enthusiastic cooperation of his clients. William Davidson and his family had for some time been patrons of Mackintosh's work, commissioning furniture and decorative work prior to the Windyhill project. WW Blackie, on the other hand, was introduced to Mackintosh by Talwin Morris, art director of Blackie's publishing firm and a friend of the architect. Other clients included Jessie (Mrs Francis) Newbery's family, the Rowats of Kingsborough Gardens; Mackintosh's future in-laws at Dunglass Castle, Bowling, and Catherine Cranston, for whom Mackintosh remodelled Hous' Hill (where she lived with her husband, Major John Cochrane) and provided numerous tea-room schemes.

The interiors Mackintosh and his wife designed for their flat at 120 Mains Street and their second home in Southpark Avenue confirm their concept of the ideal living environment unimpeded by the wishes of a client. The decorative scheme for the first – of which only photographs remain – established a pattern reflected in the recently reconstructed interiors of the second (in the Hunterian Art Gallery, Glasgow) and all his subsequent interior projects. In general terms, drawing rooms and bedrooms would be dark, and all furniture, furnishings and light fittings would be specially designed to harmonize with the setting. With plain walls, floors and ceilings, rooms were sparsely furnished and spacious compared to the fashionable clutter of most middle-class homes at that time.

The effect of these interiors was captured by Mary Newbery Sturrock, who described the Mackintoshes' drawing room at 78 Southpark Avenue in the following way: 'The room was always very simple giving an impression of withdrawn quiet and repose – nothing lay about accidentally – every single thing in the room was carefully considered, down to the smallest detail – even grey corduroy cushions, one on each side of the fireplace fender for their grey Persian cats'. It was this concept of the room as a whole – within which and to which all minor elements were related – that so distinguished Mackintosh's work and, together with his preference for broad, plain surfaces, had such far-reaching effects upon future developments.

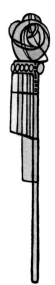

The Drawing Room, Hill House. The stencilled briar rose motif is echoed in Margaret Macdonald's gesso panel which hangs above the fireplace.

Equal care was given to the overall sequence of rooms. In Southpark Avenue a delicate balance of contrasting and complementary interiors was achieved passing from the narrow hallway with its cool tonality of white, grey-brown and black, to the dining room with its dark-stained furniture and stencilled brown walls, to the L-shaped studio-drawing room where the predominantly white colour scheme created a breathtakingly light interior.

This sensitivity towards an interior environment recalls accounts given of the English designer EW Godwin's decorative schemes for the home he shared with Ellen Terry, the actress, in the 1870s. In 1884 Godwin designed what must have been one of the earliest 'white' interiors for the poet Oscar Wilde. The subtle gradations of white he employed were inspired by Japanese prints, as were the tonal gradations of the paintings of James Abbott McNeill Whistler, for whom Godwin had designed the White House in Tite Street, Chelsea, some seven years earlier.

The extraordinary white settings of Mackintosh's home provided the ideal backdrop to his furniture and carefully placed decorative touches – small groups of ceramics, glass bottles, Japanese prints and Oriental flower arrangements of dried gypsophila and clematis. The dark interior of his dining room was no less unusual though different in character: sombre and even mysterious to suit the important ritual of eating and drinking, the grey-brown walls were offset by stencilled decoration in maroon, silver and green, a rich background for the paintings and repoussé metalwork of the interior.

Stencilling was an art practised by many designers of the period; it was a traditional form of wall decoration in Scotland, and was readily adapted to fabric and woodwork. Stencilled designs were often employed by Mackintosh to establish a harmonious scheme within an interior. At Hill House a simple stencilled design, in delicate tints of green and rose and repeating rhythmically around the drawing room, introduces a favourite theme of the briar rose, echoed in the stencilled pattern of the original window-seat upholstery and in the gesso panel and embroidered decoration by Margaret Macdonald. In the hallway a series of stencilled designs, con-

sisting of chequerboard squares, curves, ovoids and tendril-like forms, creates a distinctive frieze; the colours purple, blue, pink and green are repeated in the original carpet, with squares grouped around its perimeter.

Other devices employed by Mackintosh as wall and floor coverings were of particular interest. The dining room walls in his Mains Street flat were apparently covered to picture-rail level with coarse brown wrapping paper, while light grey canvas was used in the drawing room, with white woodwork cover strips and a frieze rail decorated with gesso insets. Gesso panels were combined with gold leaf and used as an exotic wall covering for the Cochrane's card room at Hous'Hill. For floor coverings in his own homes, Mackintosh tended to favour simple grey or rich brown fitted carpeting; elsewhere rugs or carpets resembling the type used for the hallway at Hill House were designed by Mackintosh to help unify his decorative commissions. Some reports tell how Mackintosh covered the drawing room floor at Southpark Avenue with sized sailcloth; sailcloth stencilled with a chequerboard pattern was also used as a stair covering and apparently

cleaned well and lasted for many years.

Distinctive features of all Mackintosh interiors were the fireplaces and fitted seating. At Dunglass Castle he designed the first of his great white mantelpieces. Seven feet (2.10 m) long and devoid of ornament, the mantelpiece sustained interest by the play of light upon its series of square pigeonholes. Most of his subsequent fireplaces follow this pattern, often with simple cottage-type hob grates with plain surrounds occasionally inset with tiles or coloured-glass mosaics for decorative effect. High-backed fitted seats often were located in the corner adjacent to the fireplace or in a nearby alcove. The window seat in the Hill House drawing room is a particularly fine example; with magazine racks on either side, it completely fills the window bay, offering superb views over the garden and beyond. Also at Hill House, Mackintosh designed an impressive set of fitted wardrobes for the main bedroom, while the service quarters contain what must be some of the earliest fitted kitchen units.

By concentrating on the furniture and decorative aspects of these interiors, it is easy to over-

ABOVE The Drawing Room, Hill House. A stencilled design in delicate tints of green and rose unifies this large and spatially complex room.

ABOVE The Hall, Hill House. An impressive frieze of stencilled designs interspersed with straps of dark stained pine introduces a rhythmic pattern. These colours and detailing are repeated elsewhere in the furniture, carpet and light fittings.

RIGHT The Bedroom, Hill House. High-backed corner seating provided an intimate atmosphere in this section of the bedroom, intended to function as a morning room.

OVERLEAF The Bedroom, Hill House. Natural and artificial light sources and a complex series of spatial relationships were carefully orchestrated in Mackintosh's interiors. A vaulted ceiling echoed in a curve in the outside wall adjacent to the bed helps to distinguish the separate functions of this section of the room.

look Mackintosh's adept handling of natural and artificial light. In his own drawing rooms he used tightly-stretched white muslin window screens and curtains to soften any strong sunlight, at the same time taking care to maximize the subtle play of reflected light from the white walls, fireplace and furniture. The artificial lighting in his interiors would have been conspicuously subdued compared to modern standards. The bulbs then in use were only of 25 or 50 watts and the enclosed metal or coloured-glass shades favoured by Mackintosh cast a downward light, while the room was softly illuminated by reflected light and coloured shadows.

Mackintosh similarly orchestrated the spatial relationships in his interiors with masterly precision. By ingenious planning he created a room for the Blackies which functioned both as a music room and a drawing room and could be transformed according to the occasion or the season. Separate bays, uncarpeted and with low ceilings, were designed to accommodate the piano and window seat, allowing for musical evenings and giving a focus to the room in summer; in winter a couch was drawn towards the fireplace to create a more enclosed draught-free environment. The bedroom at Hill House was similarly designed to fulfil more than one function. When the elaborate glazed screen intended to separate the two parts of the L-shaped room was rejected, Mackintosh devised an alternative. Two black chairs were used, their position and appearance serving as a visual punctuation in the softer white surroundings of the rest of the room.

While working on domestic commissions

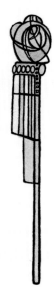

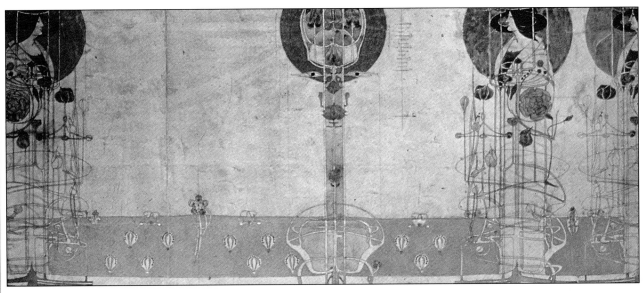

Mackintosh was simultaneously working on Catherine Cranston's Tea Rooms. These establishments were more extensive than their name suggests. They included tea-rooms, luncheon rooms for men and women, general luncheon rooms, dinner rooms, billiard rooms and smoking rooms. They provided Mackintosh with the opportunity for creating advanced spatial experiments, as well as whimsical effects not possible in his normal interior commissions. Of all Mackintosh's decorative work nothing brought him greater fame than these remarkable interiors; indeed, few of his projects created greater interest at home and abroad.

Tea-rooms were a particularly Glaswegian phenomenon at the turn of the century. A shrewd businesswoman with a flair for the dramatic, Miss Cranston was a well established tea-room proprietress on the threshold of expansion when Mackintosh first met her in 1896. Commissioned to share with George Walton the decoration of both the Buchanan Street Tea Rooms and the Argyle Street premises, Mackintosh's earliest contribution was limited to mural decorations and furniture design. However, these two small projects marked the beginnings of a collaboration which was to extend over the next 20 years and was to provide Mackintosh with some of the most important of his tragically small range of commissions.

After 1901 Mackintosh had sole professional control over the tea-room projects. In 1901 he began work on Miss Cranston's premises in Ingram Street. These comprised a series of inter-connected apartments to which adjacent properties were gradually added. Mackintosh designed the interior for the most recent of these acquisitions and several years later re-designed earlier rooms. The first of these, the White Dining Room, was not significantly different in spirit from his domestic interiors of this period. To appreciate the distinctive style which Mackintosh evolved in these commissions, one must turn to the most accomplished of the whole series, The Willow Tea Rooms.

The Willow Tea Rooms was the only project for Miss Cranston for which Mackintosh was responsible for both interior and exterior. Whereas its narrow frontage overlooking Sauchiehall Street was deceptively simple, the manipulation of the complex series of spaces created within revealed great skill and ingenuity. Using open screens and balconies to divide and subdivide the interior, Mackintosh created three interrelated though separate apartments. A balcony to the rear of the ground-floor restaurant reduced the ceiling level and created the effect of dividing the room in two. The staircase rising from the ground floor was open, as was the edge of the gallery, from which the front section of the restaurant could be seen through a glazed and wrought-iron screen.

The decorative scheme of the Willow Tea Rooms was based on the willow-tree form, from which came the street name, Sauchiehall, or 'alley of the willows'. The theme of young willows was used throughout the decoration – in the

ABOVE Design for a stencilled mural decoration, Buchanan Street Tea Rooms, Glasgow (1896). Only this design and photographs remain of Mackintosh's imposing mural scheme in Buchanan Street. Large white-robed figures entwined in branches were disposed in groups round the walls of the general tea room on the first floor.

OPPOSITE LEFT The Peacock Study for a mural decoration in the Buchanan Street Tea Rooms, Glasgow (1897–8). In the luncheon room stylized trees and peacock motifs were employed.

71

RIGHT Room de Luxe, Willow Tea Rooms, Glasgow. Original view of the impressive leaded glass gallery and frieze. The pierced pattern of the chair backs was echoed in the soft grey carpet lined and patterned in squares of various sizes, while the Willow Pattern tea services were used to compliment the decorative theme which ran through the whole restaurant.

RIGHT Interior of the Willow Tea Rooms from the balcony showing the wrought iron balustrades and the front section of the restaurant with the white plaster wall frieze.

LEFT Front saloon of the dining room in the Willow Tea Room (1903).

BELOW The Dining Room in Willow Tea Rooms showing staircase, balcony and view through to the rear section of this room on the ground floor.

stylized patterns of embroidered and stencilled panels, decorative ironwork, a plaster frieze and various fittings. The culmination of this 'symbolism' was a gesso panel by Margaret Mackintosh inspired by Rossetti's sonnet, 'O ye, all ye that walk in the willow wood.'

Colour was usually only used by Mackintosh in small touches of intense hue. Continued use' was made of light and dark to aid spatial articulation. On entering the Willow Tea Rooms the visitor was greeted by an expanse of white walls and tablecloths contrasting with dark-stained furniture and the darker interior beyond. In the Room de Luxe a more daring colour scheme was introduced, using silver-painted chairs with purple upholstery, purple silk panels on the walls, silvered mirrors, and purple and white glass. In the Chinese Room in the Ingram Street premises, Mackintosh completely abandoned his normally restrained palette for a vivid combination of bright blues and sombre reds.

Mackintosh's interiors became increasingly adventurous and accomplished from 1907 to 1911. The decorative schemes devised for the Chinese Room and the Cloister Room of the Ingram Street Tea Rooms marked the beginnings of a style perfected five years later in 78 Derngate, Northampton. The ingenious fantasy of the Chinese Room is particularly interesting. The rectilinear emphasis of the extensive lattice-work screens was relieved by the fretwork decoration elsewhere. Around the room, spaces between the lattice frame were filled with concave niches. The subtle colours and reflective surfaces of these combined with the subdued lighting, blue paintwork and dark oak furniture to give the room a mysterious and exotic quality.

ABOVE The Drawing Room, Hill House. A particularly fine example of fitted seating, a distinctive feature of Mackintosh's interiors, designed for the bay windows.

LEFT Room de Luxe, Willow Tea Rooms, Glasgow (reconstruction). The rich purple of the upholstery was echoed with tiny accents of rose-pink and mauve enamel in the leaded mirror-glass of the frieze and door.

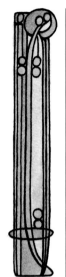

chapter five
FURNITURE, FABRIC DESIGNS, METALWORK AND GLASS

ABOVE Pair of chairs for the Dutch Kitchen (1906), a room designed and furnished by Mackintosh as a later addition to the original Argyle Street Tea Rooms.

Few of his contemporaries would have judged Mackintosh by his architectural achievements. His most important building, the Glasgow School of Art, was hardly known outside that city while the Hill House and Windyhill projects, which attracted greater publicity, were admired at least as much for their interiors and furniture as for their architectural merits. Moreover, it is clearly apparent from his commissions abroad that it was a designer of furniture fully integrated with its setting that Mackintosh earned his reputation on the Continent.

Mackintosh designed over 400 pieces of furniture in a working life of just 25 years.

Usually intended for specified environments, few of these designs would have been available through normal retail outlets. Working for private, style-conscious clients and free from commercial restraints, Mackintosh was able to expand and refine his stylistic vocabulary. His imaginative, often daring solutions to furniture design were among the most exciting of his whole oeuvre.

The best-known and most characteristic of Mackintosh's designs is the high-backed chair. Among the bold outlines and boxy shapes of the furniture commissioned for Miss Cranston's Argyle Street Tea Rooms, one chair stood out as the first of its kind. The plain wood surfaces

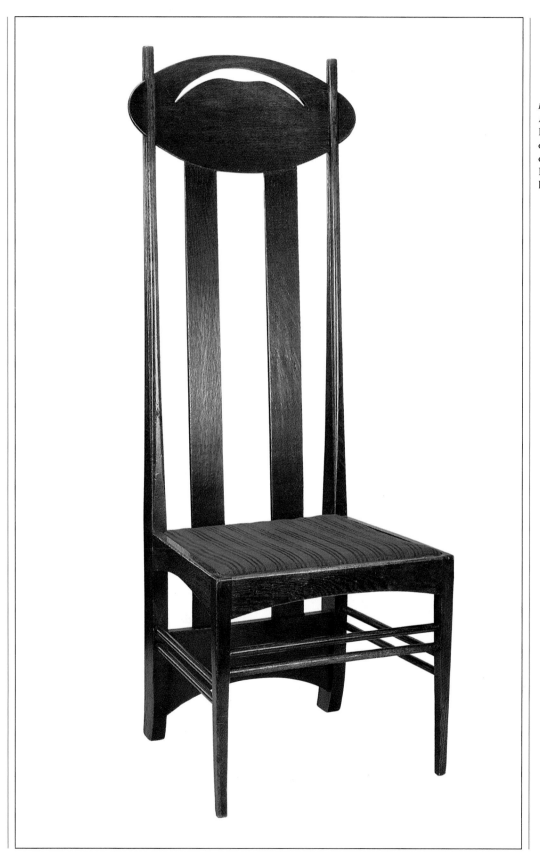

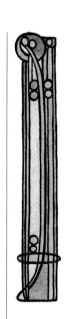

LEFT Chair for the
Argyle Street Tea
Rooms (1897). The
earliest and most
characteristic of
Mackintosh's famous
high-backed chairs.

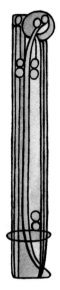

RIGHT Chair exhibited in Turin in 1902 and bought by Viennese businessman Fritz Wärndorfer.

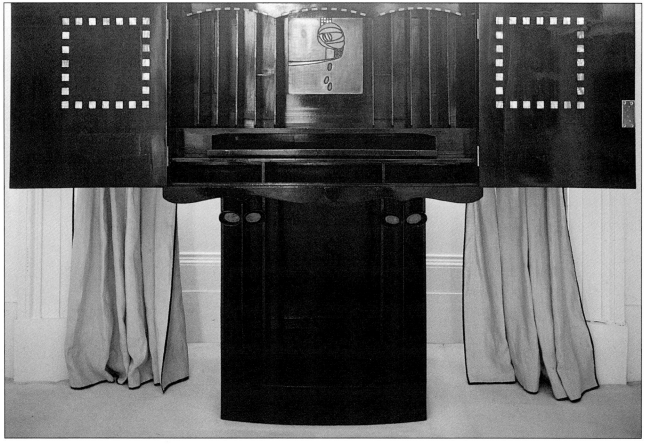

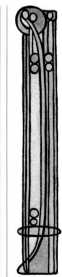

and unadorned simplicity of this chair linked it, like so many of his early pieces, to the Arts and Crafts Movement. Unlike his English contemporaries, however, Mackintosh was concerned primarily with the look of the object than its craftsmanship and comfort.

Unfortunately, high-backed chairs of this type were liable to damage when subjected to constant use in the tea-room environment; some were reinforced with metal brackets while others were reduced in height. Their tall backs did serve a particular function, however. In the crowded tea-rooms they helped to define and divide the space, their oval panels being visible over the heads of seated customers. These chairs added vertical emphasis when required: used singly or in small groups, they provided invaluable decorative elements in a large, high room; and if grouped around a table they allowed a sense of intimacy and enclosure for dining.

The theme of the high-backed chair developed far beyond functional needs, becoming a vehicle for Mackintosh's particular brand of symbolism. Echoing the attenuated, heraldic shapes in his watercolours and poster designs, the high-backed chairs for Argyle Street can be seen to resemble stylized tree forms, symbols expressive of the upward, surging vitality of so much of Mackintosh's work. It is significant that in the Willow Tea Rooms the high, spindly backs of the chairs were intended to convey the idea of a forest of young willows. References to natural motifs are perhaps more explicit in a chair exhibited at the International Exhibition of Modern Decorative Art in Turin in 1902 and bought by Viennese businessman and art patron, Fritz Wärndorfer. The tallest of the high-backed chairs, it is also one of the most decorative, with its carved organic ornamentation, white woodwork and a rose motif stencilled on its upholstery.

His furniture, like the white interiors, suggests Mackintosh's search for a new style. The more feminine and literal qualities in the decoration reflect the close collaboration between Mackintosh and Margaret Macdonald on the Rose Boudoir exhibition room at Turin. By painting wood white, black or silver,

ABOVE Writing cabinet, 1904. This was Mackintosh's own cabinet, built as duplicate of one designed for Walter W Blackie at Hill House.

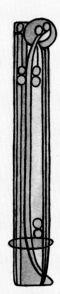

BELOW The geometric style of this chair designed for Walter Blackie marked a move away from the organic quality of the Wärndorfer chair.

RIGHT Washstand, Hill House. The subtle combination of colours and geometric shapes in the washstand are echoed in the window shutters, cheval mirror and carved decoration and glass on the wardrobes in the main bedroom. The geometric motifs which dominate the furniture at Hill House anticipate the striking simplicity of the designs at Derngate.

RIGHT
Dressing table for Derngate. The geometric style and cubic motifs first introduced in the furniture for Hill House were developed in the designs for his client Bassett Lowke at Derngate, Northampton.

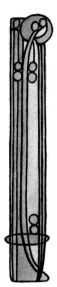

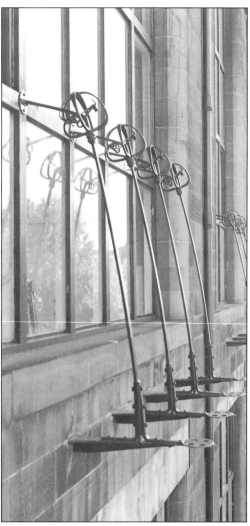

ABOVE LEFT A finial in wrought iron positioned high above the east of the School of Art and another above the main entrance interpret the Arms of the City of Glasgow.

ABOVE RIGHT Window brackets, Glasgow School of Art. Wrought iron work used in a controlled yet whimsical way relieves the severity of the Art school building. Wrought iron used in this simultaneously functional and decorative way is a feature of the School.

Mackintosh was able to release it from its traditional restrictions; by obscuring the grain and the construction of the furniture, he experimented with the concept of a more malleable medium. The delicate white-painted furniture from 1902, of which the Wärndorfer chair is a good example, created a distinctive style which Mackintosh then proceeded to react against in subsequent designs.

The low-backed chairs, which recur in a variety of forms, particularly in the tea-room projects, were on the whole more soundly constructed than those of more exaggerated proportions. Squat and cubic, they gave an impression of sturdy utility, a factor which was increasingly cultivated in Mackintosh's furniture from 1904 onwards. Simpler designs placed a renewed emphasis on unmodelled surfaces and exposed grain; organic motifs were

abandoned and chamfered edges and lattice-work motifs were adopted in their place. The wavy lines and square patterns from this period of Mackintosh's furniture design were reflected in the late decorative schemes for the Ingram Street Tea Rooms.

A transitional phase in Mackintosh's development can be pinpointed in the Hill House furniture. A writing desk and accompanying chair for WW Blackie reveal a more sophisticated application of materials and a simple, geometric use of line reflecting the move away from the organic imagery of the Wärndorfer chair. A washstand in the main bedroom combines some of Mackintosh's earliest decorative motifs with new ones. The shape of the mirror recalls the oval panel in the Argyle Street chair, while the rose in each door panel is combined with his new latticework motif, which is repeated in the

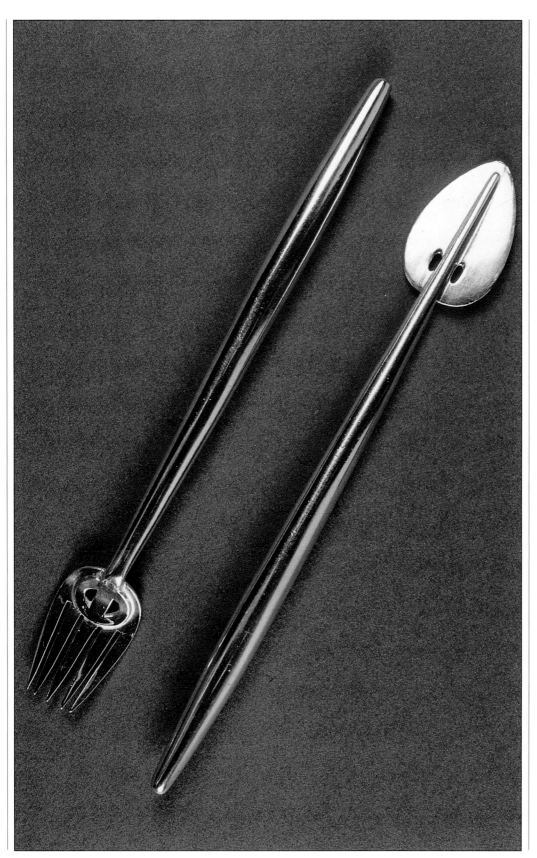

LEFT Fish knife and fork, *c*1903.

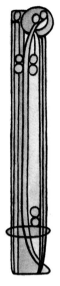

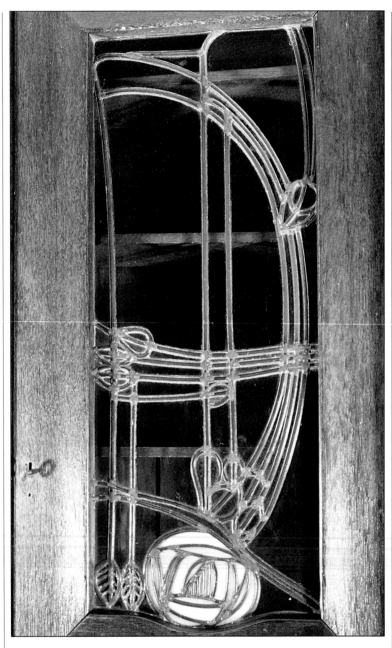

the simple shapes of the furniture. Moreover, the rigid, geometrical design, rectangular silhouettes and black-lacquered latticework of the hall furniture at Derngate is as much a hallmark of Charles Rennie Mackintosh's oeuvre as the white-painted furniture with stencilled roses of 1902.

Metalwork contributed significantly to Charles Rennie Mackintosh's output. From the design of individual handcrafted caskets and repoussé panels to the realization of wrought iron's decorative potential in the Willow Tea Rooms, metalwork was employed by Mackintosh in a number of ways. For his earliest furniture he designed simple metal locks, handles and hinges (usually broad, tapering bands ending in a leaf-shaped ornament). These simple fittings were soon combined with repoussé panels as Margaret Macdonald collaborated with him on metalwork incorporated into his furniture. Later, cutlery and cruets were designed for Miss Cranston's Tea Rooms, as well as light fittings for the School of Art and other commissions.

ABOVE A leaded glass panel of stylized roses for a stained oak cabinet, a device commonly employed by Mackintosh and other Glasgow Style designers. Coloured and leaded glass incorporated into furniture helped to compliment the colour scheme of a room.

splashback's subtle play of squares and rectangles of coloured glass. The geometric motifs which dominate the furniture at Hill House set the style for the striking simplicity of the Derngate designs in Northampton, Mackintosh's last major commission.

Mackintosh's later furniture is often considered heavy and uncharacteristic. In fact, it marked a return to some of his earliest ideas first used for Argyle Street Tea Rooms, with geometric motifs introduced to counteract heavy broad planes of natural timber and emphasize

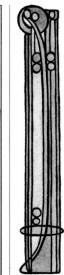

One of the most striking features of the School of Art is the way in which architectural ironwork is used in a functional yet decorative way. Wrought-iron brackets, which serve as window bracing and as supports for window cleaning, also form an attractive foil to the otherwise uncompromising austerity of the exterior. Ironwork accorded Mackintosh the opportunity to endow the building with its own unique symbolism. A finial in wrought iron positioned high above the east front, and another above the main entrance, depict a stylized re-creation of the bird-in-a-tree motif emblematic of the city of Glasgow. At the Art School and in the Tea Rooms Mackintosh exploited the linear potential of wrought iron, working in a controlled yet whimsical manner which closely resembled his work with pen and paper.

Glass was similarly used to great effect. In the Mackintoshes' Mains Street flat, the white furniture was relieved by inlays of purple, rose and green glass, which coordinated with stencilled hangings of the same colours. Glass squares were inserted into furniture and interior fittings alike – walls and doors, window shutters and fireplace surrounds. Panels of leaded glass were employed in furniture, or as decorative pendants (the latter can be seen hanging from several of the tea-room fireplaces in contemporary photographs).

At Windyhill Mackintosh experimented with glass in a fireplace surround of rich golden mosaic, inset with five small circular rose motifs of coloured glass and enamel. Insets of this type were employed at Hill House and on many subsequent occasions. Glass was used in a particularly inventive way in a fireplace at Hous'hill. Reports tell of a large fireplace in the card room which, instead of the usual plaster, mosaic or tiled surround, had a surround of thick plate glass set horizontally, with rough edges slightly projecting. The result was a scintillating effect of liquid green, particularly attractive at night, often remarked upon and well remembered by many who visited the house.

Perhaps the most famous of Mackintosh's creations in glass was the extraordinary doorway for the Room de Luxe in the Willow Tea

ABOVE Bookcase, 1900. The leaded glass door panels of these bookcases for Mackintosh's own home were a *tour de force* and one of the most elegant designs in glass that he was to produce.

OPPOSITE RIGHT Mackintosh incorporated metalwork into his furniture in the form of ornamental repoussé panels. This one comes from a stained oak cabinet.

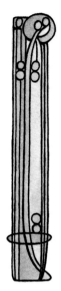

RIGHT Orange and Purple Spirals. Plant forms often gave Mackintosh a starting point for his textile designs. In this one, natural forms of stems and tendrils are stylized to form striking abstract patterns in this design.

OPPOSITE PAGE Pink Tobacco Flower. This unusual textile design was traced from the hair of a figure in *The Opera of the Sea* by Margaret Macdonald Mackintosh. A number of finished designs for textiles were developed from this drawing.

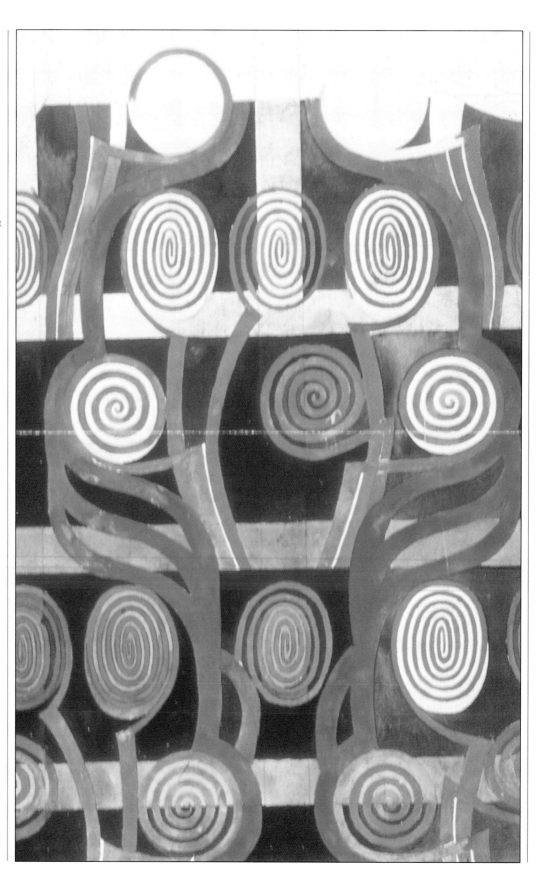

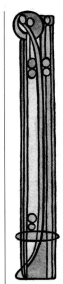

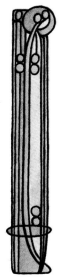

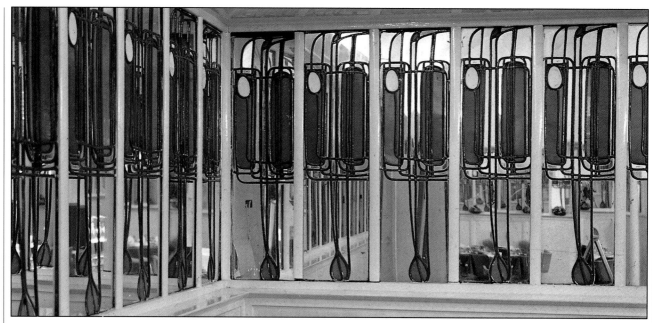

ABOVE In this mirrored and stained glass frieze from the Room de Luxe (Willow Tea Rooms) Mackintosh employed a stylized willow motif and colours to compliment those used elsewhere in the room.

Rooms. The most elaborate and certainly the largest of his designs in leaded glass, it formed only part of this project's dazzling scheme. Around the edges of the room ran a frieze of leaded mirror-glass panels with tiny accents of rose-pink and mauve enamel, echoing the purple-upholstered furniture. The theme of the frieze, and throughout the tea-room, was the willow, with stylized leaves and waving stems, combined with Mackintosh's favourite motif of the rose. In the centre of the room, a crystal chandelier was suspended from the low arched ceiling, forming a glittering cluster of glass balls, ovals and teardrops which both reflected the light and cast evocative shadows.

Designing for printed fabrics was a new departure for Mackintosh – any previous designs of this sort had been stencilled or embroidered in appliqué. When the Mackintoshes were living in Chelsea during World War I and architectural work was unavailable, both began to work freelance for two leading London textile firms, Foxton's and Sefton's. He produced designs at the price of £5 and £20 each; this was the first time that Mackintosh had designed for a more general market.

A large group of his original drawings for textiles have survived. In these Mackintosh developed a whole new vocabulary, linked to his Glasgow work, yet anticipating the major decorative style of the 1920s, Art Deco. Earlier linear designs of tendrils and roses, in which

space played such a vital role, were replaced by densely crowded patterns based on stylized plant forms or abstract, geometric shapes. All were rendered in vivid shades of red, yellow, blue, green and purple. Only a few fabrics survive to indicate what these stunning designs must have looked like when made up into lengths for curtains, dresses or upholstery.

The fabric designs were often developed from elements in Charles's or Margaret's paintings. For example, 'Blue and Pink Tobacco Flowers' is taken from a detail in Margaret's decorative panel, *The Opera of the Sea*. While keeping the basic motif, Mackintosh reorganized the structure of the design to produce a lively, yet harmonious pattern for fabric. Mackintosh gave three different colourways, showing how easily and dramatically the whole effect may be altered by a simple change of hue.

It is difficult to gauge the success of these designs at the time, but Mackintosh seemed to have been earning a creditable wage (his and Margaret's combined income for 1920 alone was some £200). Despite this, he was becoming increasingly depressed and melancholic. His architectural designs were rejected and success as a graphic or textile designer could not compensate for his frustrated architectural ambitions. The textile designs themselves give no hint of Mackintosh's state of mind, however: they are consistently bright and colourful, testaments to his mastery of form, line and colour.

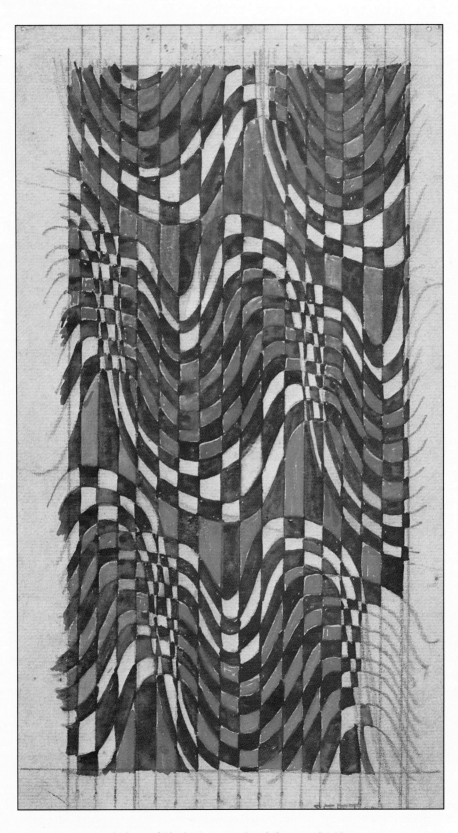

ABOVE Stripes and Checks. A conventional chequered grid pattern
is distorted by introducing wavy lines to form an unusual and striking textile.

chapter six

MACKINTOSH ABROAD

ABOVE Maison and Atelier Horta, Brussels, 1898, Victor Horta (1861–1947). Although the origins of Art Nouveau may be found in Britain, it came to be regarded largely as a Continental style due in part to the work of Victor Horta and Henry van de Velde working in the fast-expanding Belgian capital.

U nlike the Arts and Crafts Movement, Art Nouveau was a clearly defined and conscious attempt to evolve a style entirely independent of tradition — wood and metal were contorted into the most extravagant shapes; structure disappeared beneath a mass of soft, undulating lines. Brussels and Paris were the centres of the new style; Victor Horta's Maison Tassel (1892–93) and Hôtel Solvay (1894–95), both in Brussels, gave architectural form to the movement, as did Hector Guimard's numerous Parisian projects, while Henry Van de Velde's writings and lectures proved an excellent form of publicity. After a commission from the influential German-born art dealer S Bing to decorate and furnish several apartments in his shop, La Maison de l'Art Nouveau (which gave the style its name), in the Rue de Provence, Paris, Van de Velde's work began to attract considerable attention and the Belgian quickly secured an influential following. His work was exhibited in Dresden and provided the impetus for a group of young artists there to establish their own German version of the style, known as 'Jugendstil'.

By the end of the century Art Nouveau was firmly entrenched in Europe; it had reached Warsaw, Breslau, Dresden, Prague, Darmstadt, Munich, Vienna and Budapest. But the British journals carried little evidence of the exciting artistic events abroad, this largely due to the strong position which Arts and Crafts design still held in England. In an attack in the publication *Our Homes and How to Beautify Them* — sponsored by London furniture makers Waring & Gillow and containing a chapter, 'L'Art Nouveau on the Continent' with reproductions of a Mackintosh interior – an anonymous author wrote: '... The Scotto-Continental "New Art" threatens with its delirious fantasies to make the movement for novelty a target for

ABOVE Staircase, Maison et Atelier Horta, Brussels, 1898. The 'whiplash' line which typifies Art Nouveau was developed in an architectural context by Victor Horta, notably in staircase designs for buildings like Hotel Tassel and the Maison et Atelier Horta.

RIGHT Poster
advertising the annual
exhibition held by the
Vienna Secession.
Formed in opposition to
the more conservative
Academy, the Secession
was an independent
exhibiting society whose
members included
architects Josef
Hoffmann and JM
Olbrich and the painter
Gustav Klimt.

OPPOSITE RIGHT Cover
for the lithographic
portfolio of
Mackintosh's entry for
the Haus eines
Kunstfreundes (House of
an Art Lover)
competition.

RIGHT The Secession
Building, Vienna,
1897–98 by JM Olbrich.
In 1900 the
Mackintoshes were
invited to Vienna to
supervise the
decoration and
furnishing of a room
setting in the annual
Secessionist exhibition.

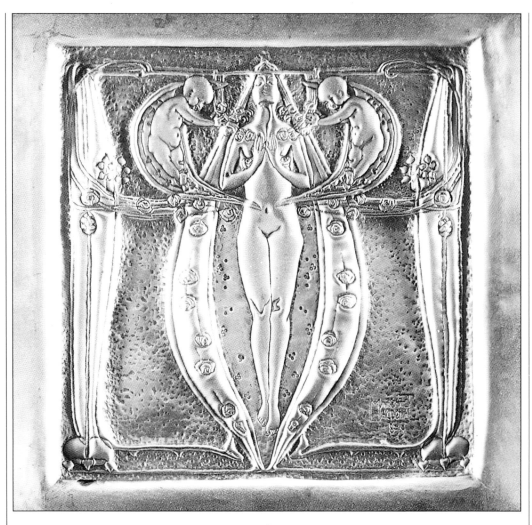

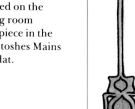

LEFT Metal panel by Margaret Macdonald Mackintosh, 1899. Originally forming part of a firescreen exhibited at Vienna, this panel was subsequently displayed on the drawing room mantelpiece in the Mackintoshes Mains Street flat.

the shafts of scoffers . . .' The critic continued: 'The authors of these dreadful designs, lacking artistic inventiveness, have been driven to seek originality in fantastic forms remote from any connection with Art'.

To help assess Mackintosh's position with regard to Art Nouveau and other turn-of-the-century developments on the Continent, it is necessary first to examine his work abroad. Contrary to popular opinion, Mackintosh did not undertake any architectural projects on the Continent; the three documented commissions were relatively minor, in the decorative sphere and for private individuals. However, his work aroused great enthusiasm and was widely publicized in foreign journals. It was first illustrated in an article on the Glasgow group in Alexander Koch's *Dekorative Kunst* in November 1898. The May 1899 issue of the same publication showed a photograph of a furnished dining

room by Mackintosh. There is no evidence that Mackintosh visited Europe in the 19th century, other than his scholarship tour in 1891; however, in 1900 this was to change radically.

In the late autumn of 1900 The Four were invited to furnish and decorate an entire room in the Secessionist Exhibition in Vienna. Their work went on to be exhibited in Munich, Dresden, Budapest and elsewhere. In 1901 Mackintosh submitted a scheme for the famous 'Haus eines Kunstfreundes' competition and designed a music salon in Vienna for Fritz Wärndorfer. In 1902 the Mackintoshes showed at the International Exhibition of Modern Decorative Art at Turin. Numerous visits to Vienna were undertaken, and each time the Mackintoshes were greeted with great enthusiasm and hailed as leaders of the new movement.

The Secession was an independent society, formed· after a number of exhibitions of

ABOVE Emile Flöge by Gustav Klimt. The most prominent artist of the Secession, producing paintings, murals and wall panels in a highly decorative style which was both influenced by and influential upon the work of Mackintosh.

modern work had been bitterly opposed by the more conservative Viennese Academy. Among the founding members were the architects Josef Hoffman and JM Olbrich, and the painters Gustav Klimt, Carl Moll and Felician von Myrbach. The veteran painter Rudolf von Alt was elected leader of the group. These men, already familiar with or even influenced by Scottish painting and design, invited Charles and Margaret to visit Vienna to supervise the decoration and furnishing of an apartment allocated to them in the 'Secession House', which had been designed by Olbrich two years previously.

The exhibits consisted largely of pieces from the Mains Street flat or borrowed from Miss Cranston's Ingram Street Tea Rooms. Mackintosh must have been astonished and highly gratified to discover a group of artists and designers who were not only sympathetic to his views but had themselves evolved an equivalent style. He prepared the apartment allocated to The Four in characteristic style. Framed gesso panels were the dominant feature, with the walls beneath divided into broad panels between freestanding tapered columns carrying a broad cornice; for variation a deep rail was introduced, pierced at intervals by square insets, each containing a coloured-glass panel with a strong curvilinear pattern. The entire room was painted white. The furniture was mainly of Mackintosh's own design – two oak cabinets with decorative metal and leaded-glass panels, two high-backed chairs, a tall white-painted cheval mirror, candle sconces, pedestal, flower vase, paintings and embroidered fabrics.

The exhibition was a great success for Mackintosh. The all-pervading whiteness of the room and its careful arrangement of furniture created a unified effect which was new and exciting to the Viennese. Their influence can be seen in the designs submitted by the Secessionists to later exhibitions, many of whose earlier exhibitions had been crowded and badly presented. The two gesso panels may have influenced Gustav Klimt in his own later contribution to the Fourteenth Exhibition of the Vienna Secession, the *Beethoven Frieze*. The only pieces to remain in Vienna were an oval-backed armchair, which was bought by architect-designer Koloman Moser, and Mackintosh's smoker's cabinet, bought by Hugo Henneberg. Despite the few sales – and the fact that the

LEFT Cheval Mirror, 1900. Painted oak with glass inserts and silvered brass handles. The most elaborate of its kind to be designed by Mackintosh, this mirror was exhibited in Vienna at the Secessionist exhibition.

Hoffmann was a prolific designer of chairs, much influenced by Mackintosh. The chairs (*ABOVE*), whose backs are a pastiche of a Sheraton tea tray, are a good example of his bentwood furniture, as is the Biach chair (*RIGHT*). This design was light and economical to produce yet stylish and sturdy.

exhibition resulted in very few direct commissions – it was undoubtedly a triumph for Mackintosh, who had forged links with men like Hoffman, Klimt, Moser and Wärndorfer and who had established himself as a major European designer. A whole generation of students was exposed to his work; they began to evolve their own style based on white paint, colour inlays and, most importantly, the use of the square as a dominant decorative motif.

Mackintosh, Josef Hoffman and the other Secessionists shared common objectives. Hoffman and Mackintosh became good friends, the Austrian visiting the Mackintoshes in Glasgow; Fritz Wärndorfer followed in 1902. These two men, along with Koloman Moser, were to establish the Wiener Werkstätte (Viennese Workshops), a school of design and craft, in

1902. Mackintosh was invited to set up a studio and metal workshop in Vienna. Although he turned this offer down, it demonstrates the high esteem in which he was held on the Continent. Indeed, it was reported that when Charles and Margaret first arrived in Vienna the students met them at the station and, as a sign of their respect and admiration, drew them through the city in a flower-decked carriage. It was the first time that Mackintosh felt his work to have been understood and appreciated. His designs were enthusiastically received by artists and public alike, and Mackintosh returned to Scotland full of hopes, determined to establish his new vision.

The major Viennese project undertaken by Mackintosh after the Secessionist Exhibition was the Music Salon for Fritz Wärndorfer (1902). The salon was another white room, with lavender- and rose-coloured accents, similar to the interiors of Hill House and the Mains Street flat, but with the addition of a wall frieze of gesso panels and two other such panels mounted on the piano – all of these by Margaret. The most impressive item in the room was the case of the grand piano. It was over three feet (about one metre) high and nearly seven feet (two metres) square, a massive piece of furniture. The upper part was solid and decorated with Mackintosh's favourite motif of a stylized flying bird in high relief. The whole construction was supported on enormous legs which contrasted with the slender 18-inch (46-cm) rods of the music stand, each of which was capped with a small cube. The general arrangement of the room was square, with two rectangular projections on adjacent walls – one for the fireplace, the other for a large window seat. The fireplace bay projected into the room, creating its own ceiling at picture-rail height. The window was similarly enclosed, but this time in a heart-shaped arch which linked the backs of the fitted seats. The room was panelled to a height of about 6½ ft (2 m) with white-painted boards; coloured glass boxes, which no doubt contained light fittings, were positioned above alternate panels. Overhead illumination was provided by clusters of clear glass globes hung from a metal rail fixed to the ceiling.

The Music Salon became a place of pilgrimage for connoisseurs. AS Levetus, Viennese correspondent for *The Studio*, described it thus: 'The composition forms an organic whole, each

part fitting into the rest with the same concord as do the passages of a grand symphony; each thought resolves itself as do the chords in music, till the orchestration is perfect, the effect of complete repose filling the soul'.

It is an inestimable tragedy that, apart from a few ageing photographs, nothing of the Wärndorfer Music Salon is known to have survived. The story is all too familiar: after the sale of Wärndorfer's house, the contents were disposed of; the music salon was purchased by a gentleman for his daughter. The daughter soon tired of the interior and transferred everything to her loft, where it was speedily chopped up; only the gesso panels were saved by a certain Herr Wimmer, who is believed to have been associated with the Arts and Crafts Museum in Vienna. These panels were subsequently exhibited in the museum, but any trace of them has since disappeared.

In 1900 the competition to design a house for a connoisseur of the arts was announced in Alexander Koch's magazine, *Zeitschrift für Innendekoration*. It is likely that Mackintosh became aware of the competition during his stay in Vienna (JM Olbrich was one of the judges). Mackintosh's scheme aroused great interest; he was awarded a special prize of 600 marks and his drawings were reproduced in one of the folios of competition drawings published in 1902. No first prize was awarded, although the second prize was given to MH Baillie Scott, the English architect whose work satisfied the contemporary demand for a romantic mixture of gables, high-pitched roofs and dormers.

A close examination of Mackintosh's drawings for the project is highly rewarding. He was never given the opportunity to build on this scale, so the renderings are therefore indicative of his potential genius, never fulfilled due to lack of serious commissions. In the 'Haus eines Kunstfreundes', Mackintosh united the architectural qualities he had developed in Windyhill with the decorative and spatial qualities of his interior work. The simple architectural form is reflected in the elevational treatment, with broad, unbroken surfaces dominating. Some modelling is achieved in the north façade, but the south elevation consists of a simple plane. The disposition of the windows is typically informal.

The spatial organization of the house was handled with great skill. The visitor would

ABOVE The Scottish section at the Turin Exhibition, Herbert and Frances McNair.

ABOVE The Rose Boudoir, Turin, CR Mackintosh and MM Mackintosh.

move from the tiny hallway into a sudden expanse of space as he entered the two-storey, galleried hall (32 feet by 22 feet/9.75 m by 6.7 m), an idea developed from the entrance of the Glasgow School of Art. The dining room opened directly off the hall, separated by a light movable partition, as did the reception and music rooms. These last were designed *en suite*, connected with the hall by wide double doors; the whole, if desired, could be combined into one magnificent space. The hall and dining room were lined in rich, dark oak, lit by the northern light which was so close to Mackintosh's heart. By contrast the reception and music room, on the south side, were painted white and filled with light. No room was considered an entity in itself, but rather each was viewed as one element in a continual pattern of solid and void, plane and line resulting in a totally integrated spatial whole. A special room was provided for the ladies and another for the gentlemen – the former was an elegant oval, Mackintosh's favourite feminine symbol, the latter a more masculine rectangle. The staircase formed a central feature, rising directly from the hall to form a semicircular bay. Apart from the playroom in the east, all the other first-floor rooms ran off a long corridor on the south side of the building.

Alongside the architectural drawings, Charles and Margaret produced a number of designs for interiors and furniture. Their interiors were very different from those of Baillie Scott – rather than surfaces rich in ornament they preferred dark stain or white paint, which brought out the innate beauty of the material; ie, its surface texture or form. Complex patterns and rich colours were avoided except in small areas to give emphasis. For the dining room Mackintosh decided on an austere arrangement of dark walls and furniture. The whole composition is lightened by the extensive use of stencilled panels on the walls and cupboards and the simple white curved ceiling. The music and reception room was the most ornate room Mackintosh had so far designed. The entire room reflects the influence of Margaret, who designed the stencilled or embroidered panels in the window bays. At the west end of the room stands a piano or organ, which is based on the organ made for an earlier scheme in which Mackintosh was involved for Craigie Hall, Glasgow. It is an elaborate design combining motifs of birds, trees and flowers. The music room attracted the most attention of all the interior views and it is likely to have inspired Wärndorfer to commission Mackintosh to design the music room for his own house.

The major significance of the scheme was that it was the first time that a complete architectural project by Mackintosh, one in which he had been free to express himself as he wished, was made available to architects throughout Europe. The project had an incalculable in-

fluence on the future development of architecture in Europe and established Mackintosh abroad not only as a renowned decorator and furniture designer, but also as an architect.

In 1902 an International Exhibition of Modern Decorative Art was held in Turin, with the intention of drawing together the best examples of art and craftwork Europe had to offer. Francis Newbery was appointed a delegate in charge of the supervision of the Scottish section. He immediately placed the decorative schemes and layout in the hands of Mackintosh, who skilfully transformed the corridor-like area allocated into a single unified space. The decorative scheme of the rooms further emphasized this unity; panelled with white-painted woodwork and canvas, with the upper parts of the walls and ceiling whitewashed, they engendered an atmosphere of tranquillity and calm. The three rooms had themes: the first, decorated by the Mackintoshes, was known as the 'Rose Boudoir'; the second was a writing room containing the work of the MacNairs, its grey walls stencilled with an ornate frieze, its furniture black-stained oak; and the third consisted of a general exhibition of Glasgow work, ranging from bookbindings to fireplaces.

In contrast to the general hotch-potch of objects and styles at Turin, the Scottish section stood out as being not only innovative but also well designed; Fra Newbery was received by the King of Italy, the Mackintoshes were awarded diplomas and Jessie M King received a gold medal and five silver medals.

After Turin the Mackintoshes supposedly sent work to Venice, Munich, Budapest and Dresden. In 1913 they were invited by the Grand Duke Serge of Russia to exhibit in Russia under Imperial patronage. Their work was apparently received enthusiastically by artists and public alike, with everything being sold apart from the carpet (specially designed by Mackintosh for the exhibition).

It is clear that from the turn of the century until 1906 Mackintosh enjoyed great prestige abroad – and his architectural, interior and decorative work was widely publicized by such men as Muthesius and Koch. Tragically, World War I intervened; old friendships became alienated, valuable ties with the Continent were broken. When the war ended it became clear that the rich world encompassing Art Nouveau, the tail-end of the Arts and Crafts Movement and the creations of the Glasgow School had been superseded by the output of a new, younger generation of architects, who were primarily interested in engineering and industrial design. However, the Secessionist tradition was still maintained in Vienna by Hoffman. Sadly, when in 1929 a group of young architects invited Mackintosh to Vienna to honour him for his remarkable influence on the art and architecture of their country, they found that he had died a few months previously.

ABOVE Scottish exhibition area, International Exhibition of Decorative Art, Turin, 1902. Mackintosh's decorative schemes at Turin created an atmosphere of quiet and repose. In this section, selected designers' work was exhibited in a room setting and display cases specially designed by Mackintosh.

THE GLASGOW STYLE

'Nowhere has the modern movement of art been entered upon more seriously than at Glasgow; the church, the school, the house, the restaurant, the shop, the poster, the book, with its printing, illustrating and binding, have all come under the spell of the new influence.'
– The Studio, *1907*

Charles Rennie Mackintosh was not working in a vacuum, but in a city which nurtured an abundance of creative activity in the period from 1890 to 1920. The 'new influence' referred to here was Art Nouveau and its local variant, the Glasgow Style. Each city associated with Art Nouveau had its representative designer (or designers): Guimard in Paris, Emile Gallé and Louis Majorelle in Nancy, Gaudí in Barcelona, Hoffman and Moser in Vienna, Horta in Brussels, Louis Comfort Tiffany in New York and Mackintosh in Glasgow. In each case, of course, there were less well-known designers and craftworkers who played a significant role in developing and perpetuating the style.

Although the earliest examples of Art Nouveau occurred within the English Arts and Crafts Movement, its members refused to recognize the fully fledged style which subsequently swept across Europe and North America. Why, then, did Glasgow adopt this style so derided in the south? In the 1890s Glasgow was at the height of its powers; with a proud industrial heritage, it was rightly described as the Second City of the Empire. Eager to endorse its already powerful position, Glasgow recognized the advantages of a forceful cultural identity. With a characteristic flair for self-promotion and a strong commercial instinct, the city welcomed all that was new and original in the arts – the more distinctive and individual, the better. The overtly decorative style of Art Nouveau proved perfect, and the fact that it was disliked in England only served to increase its popularity in Glasgow.

The public face of architecture was an ideal vehicle for the dissemination of the new style.

Ever since the unorthodox buildings of Alexander 'Greek' Thomson, with their exotic blend of Greek and Egyptian forms, Glasgow had played host to a variety of ambitious architectural schemes. Partners James Salmon II and John Gaff Gillespie were among those who contributed to the Art Nouveau style in architecture, while the early collaboration of Mackintosh and George Walton on Miss Cranston's tea-room interiors showed how the style could be used in the city's commercial and retail environments. It is interesting to note that Walton, at the young age of 21, gave up a secure job to set up his own firm and continue such decorative work, a good indication that the time was ripe for this new style of design in Glasgow.

Not surprisingly, there was a demand for art furnishings in a city where the interest in art – cultivated by dealers like Alex Reid – encouraged a widespread enthusiasm for this too-often neglected area of human endeavour. As the younger brother of EA Walton, one of the Glasgow Boys, George Walton must have been aware of the artistic climate in Glasgow at the time and of the growing demand among collectors for contemporary works of art. Work by the Hague School and Barbizon artists was much sought after, as were paintings by Courbet and Corot. Likewise, examples of Impressionist painting from France and The Netherlands and paintings by the local heroes, the Glasgow Boys, were also becoming highly desirable. The influence of Glasgow's young painters on the decorative arts was considerable, for they not only helped to create a favourable cultural climate in Glasgow but also showed that it was possible to gain international recognition.

James Guthrie, WY Macgregor, John Lavery, Joseph Crawhall, Arthur Melville and others, influenced by works in Glasgow collections and by the French painter, Jules Bastien-Lepage, evolved a vigorous type of realism. The effect on design of this Impressionist style of painting, most often associated with the Glasgow Boys, was negligible. The more decorative tendencies evident in certain works from the late 1880s, however, suggests a direct connection between the 'Glasgow School' of painting and the 'Glasgow Style' in design.

LEFT *The Druids. Bringing in the Mistletoe* by G Henry and EA Hornel, 1889. Sharing a studio in Glasgow in the 1880s, Henry and Hornel pioneered a collaborative method of working and a decorative style in paintings like *The Druids* and its companion, *The Star in the East* (1890). The mysterious imagery and ornate quality of this work, with its tall druidic figures, Celtic ornaments and bright colours interspersed with gold, proved to be widely influential on Glasgow's designers in the 1890s.

George Henry and EA Hornel's decision to collaborate on works, like *The Druids: Bringing in the Mistletoe* (1890), pioneered a method of working later adopted by The Four. With its elaborate Celtic ornament, gold paint and patches of bright colour, this painting anticipates illuminated manuscripts, metalwork and jewellery produced in the 1890s. It was Mackintosh, however, who realized the full implications of such a work. The tall, straight-backed forms of the druidic figures are echoed time and again in the shape and proportions of Mackintosh's famous chairs.

The decorative effect of *The Druids* was exploited by another Glasgow School artist, David Gauld, who converted it into a stained-glass window design. It was Gauld – a friend of Mackintosh – who painted the remarkable *St Agnes* of 1889–90. Like a Pre-Raphaelite painting in the static and wistful pose of its single elongated figure, the image is separated into simple flattened areas of luminous colour and has the appearance of a stained-glass or embroidered panel produced in Glasgow some 10 years later.

Cosmopolitan Glasgow, with its internationally renowned group of painters, provided an ideal environment for work of an ambitious and experimental nature. At the very centre of any new developments was the Glasgow School of Art, at that time enjoying the enlightened and energetic leadership of Francis Newbery. By allowing his students to experiment freely and encouraging them to look at contemporary developments in England and abroad, Newbery was a major force behind the sudden flowering of the decorative arts in Glasgow. It was Newbery who organized the earliest exhibitions

ABOVE *Music*, a stained glass panel by David Gauld. Working both as an artist and a stained glass designer, David Gauld evolved a highly individual and decorative style.

The style steadily gained momentum, and was soon employed by a wide and talented group of designers, teachers, craftworkers and architects. Many connected with the Glasgow Style belonged to the Scottish Guild of Handicraft and the Scottish Society of Art Workers, set up to encourage, exhibit and promote Scottish decorative art; and almost all were connected in some way with the Glasgow School of Art.

When the memorial stone of the new School of Art was laid in 1898 it contained an illuminated history of the school by Jessie M King, a 22-year-old student who was soon to establish herself as one of the stars of the new Glasgow movement. The evocative fairy-tale imagery and exquisite linear detail of her illustrated work, frequently reproduced in *The Studio*, won her instant success. Just as Talwin Morris did so much to publicize the Glasgow Style, using its motifs and forms in the bindings and layout of Blackie's extensive range of books, so did King's distinctive work help to popularize the Style. Cover designer, illustrator and occasional writer of over 70 books, she also taught bookbinding at the School of Art. As well as being a prolific illustrator, she was involved in other kinds of decorative work, designing wallpapers for the Glasgow furnishers of Wylie & Lochhead, textiles for Alexander Morton & Co, and an extremely successful range of jewellery for Liberty of London. In 1908 she married the designer EA Taylor and lived for a time in Paris. Forced home by the outbreak of war the couple settled in Kirkcudbright, where Jessie turned her attention to designing interiors and fabrics, and to decorating ceramics.

The decorative potential of Glasgow Style motifs was skilfully explored by other women craftworkers and designers, particularly in a type of embroidery pioneered by the Macdonald sisters and Jessie Newbery. A former student, Mrs Newbery joined her husband on the staff at the School of Art, where she established the Embroidery Department in 1894. An enthusiastic teacher, her hard work clearly paid off. In 1902 *The Studio* advised its readers to: 'Look to the Glasgow School of Art if we wish to think of today's embroidery as a thing that lives and grows and is therefore of greater value and interest than a display of archaeology in patterns and stitches'. One of the most imaginative of British embroiderers, Mrs Newbery evolved a style of embroidery – original in its colour,

of Glasgow Style work and ensured that his students were properly represented.

In the formative years of the early 1890s the most significant Glasgow Style designs were produced by The Four. MacNair's bizarre forms, the Macdonald sisters' highly individual and innovative use of motifs, and Mackintosh's extraordinary but disciplined imagination blended to create a distinctive style of work.

design and technique – which did much to perpetuate the Glasgow Style. Ann Macbeth, a former student and later head of the department, assimilated Newbery's embroidered mottoes and organic motifs, adding her own distinctive figurative work to the Glasgow Style repertoire.

Another occupation of Glasgow's artistic community around the turn of the century was metalwork. Again much of the inspiration came from Margaret and Frances Macdonald, whose repoussé metalwork had revealed the full potential of this apparently inflexible medium. An avid collector of the Macdonald sisters' decorative metalwork was Talwin Morris, much of whose own craftwork was in beaten metal. As Art Director for Blackie's publishing firm, Talwin Morris arrived in Glasgow in 1893, just as the new style was emerging. Unlike most other Glaswegian designers, he was never officially connected with the School of Art. However, as a personal friend of the Newberys and avid supporter of The Four, he became one of the chief exponents of the style. His bookbindings, graphics, furniture, stained glass and metalwork are characterized by typical Glasgow Style imagery – strong verticals, hearts and formalized roses – and by his distinctive feline motifs.

The Glasgow School of Art's Metalwork Department, with Peter Wylie Davidson at its head, played a significant role in the subsequent outpouring of art metalwork – candlesticks, caskets, mirror frames and the like. A superb technician, Davidson completed several pieces to Mackintosh's design, while the Arts and Crafts origins and Celtic motifs in his own work were to influence generations of students, many of whom, like metalworker Margaret Gilmour, set up their own studios.

In the early years the Glasgow designers appear to have been working largely for themselves or for an intimate network of friends and associates. As the Glasgow Style became increasingly popular, however, designs were commissioned and retailed by enterprising firms like Wylie & Lochhead, which astutely judged the direction in which middle-class taste was moving. The breakthrough in taste had already been made in the 1890s by smaller firms like Walton & Co and Guthrie & Wells, the latter commissioning a range of furniture by Mackintosh in 1894.

George Walton's commission in 1888 to furnish and decorate a room in Miss Cranston's first tea-room was a momentous event; not only did it launch him on his new career but also, according to *The Studio*, it marked the beginnings of the Glasgow Style. His ornate wall surfaces, decorated with stencilled floral patterns, acorns, pineapples and so forth, predate equivalent designs in Brussels by Victor Horta, usually regarded as the earliest examples of Continental Art Nouveau. His domestic commissions in Glasgow from 1890–96 set the style for a type of interior adopted and modified for a wider market by Wylie & Lochhead's trio of designers, namely EA Taylor, George Logan and John Ednie.

The wide range and distribution of Walton's work, following his decision to settle in London, did much to promote the Glasgow Style. His refitting in about 1900 of the chain of Kodak shops – from London to locations as far-flung as Brussels, Milan and Vienna – carried his influence abroad, while his range of interiors, shop fronts and exhibition stands was extended at home, with architectural commissions which directly linked the Glasgow Style with later Arts and Crafts developments in England.

At the Glasgow International Exhibition in 1901 George Walton's stand was singled out for praise. Although he was by then based in London, his work was still thought to give 'a very favourable impression of what the newer generation of decorators are doing in Glasgow'. It was Wylie & Lochhead's pavilion, however, that dominated the furnishing section, with its interiors by Taylor, Logan and Ednie attracting widespread interest. The following year these room settings were shown again at an exhibition of British Arts and Crafts in Budapest, and furniture by the same trio was sent to the International Exhibition in Turin in 1902. This, in addition to a selection of work by the Mackintoshes and the MacNairs, and a large room devoted to Talwin Morris, Jessie M King and others, combined to form a particularly coherent and extensive display of the Glasgow Style at Turin.

It was this kind of exposure that established the international reputation of the Glasgow Style. Back home in Britain, however, the style was too closely linked in the public mind with 'the Squirm', as Continental Art Nouveau was nicknamed, for it ever to be fully accepted.

chapter seven

THE
FINAL YEARS

After his triumphs in Vienna and Turin, Mackintosh returned to Glasgow determined to bring about a revival in the applied arts and in architecture – a Scottish Secession. Sadly, indifference to and ignorance of the new art proved more deeply rooted than even Mackintosh had realized. The task Mackintosh had set himself increasingly began to feel like a one-man crusade and the exacting struggle only served to embitter him. As his enthusiasm and optimism turned to anger and resentment, Mackintosh became moody and argumentative. As he saw one project after another halted by intractable authorities, he began turning to alcohol for consolation. The architect's position became all the more frustrating when compared to that of his Austrian friends. JM Olbrich was working steadily and securely under the benevolent patronage of the Grand Duke of Hesse, while Hoffman was involved with architectural projects of major importance, including the Pürkersdorf Sanatorium in Vienna (1903) and the Palais Stoclet, Brussels (built 1905–11).

Mackintosh's manner of working did not make conditions any easier. His relentless pursuit of perfection necessitated continual changes to works in progress as well as voluminous detailing, both of which exacted high demands on the time and skill of his workmen and took account of neither the clients' nor his own firm's financial position. Relations at work steadily worsened as clients began to object to the treatment they received, and threatened to take their work elsewhere. Matters came to a head in 1913, when Mackintosh resigned from Honeyman and Keppie, ostensibly in protest over an office submission to a local competition.

It has been said that Mackintosh's drinking habits contributed to the downfall of his architectural career. However, many professionals of the day were heavy drinkers and there is no

ABOVE *Fritillaria*, 1915. Pencil and watercolour.

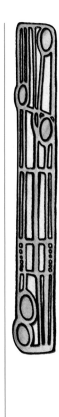

ABOVE *Larkspur*, 1914. Pencil and watercolour. It was while living in
Walberswick on the Suffolk coast that Mackintosh produced
some of the finest flower studies of his career.

RIGHT Design for a
stencilled wall
decoration for the Hall,
78 Derngate,
Northampton (1916).
This richly coloured
stencil design was
employed at intervals
throughout the room,
and can clearly be seen
above the fireplace in
the photograph of
the hall.

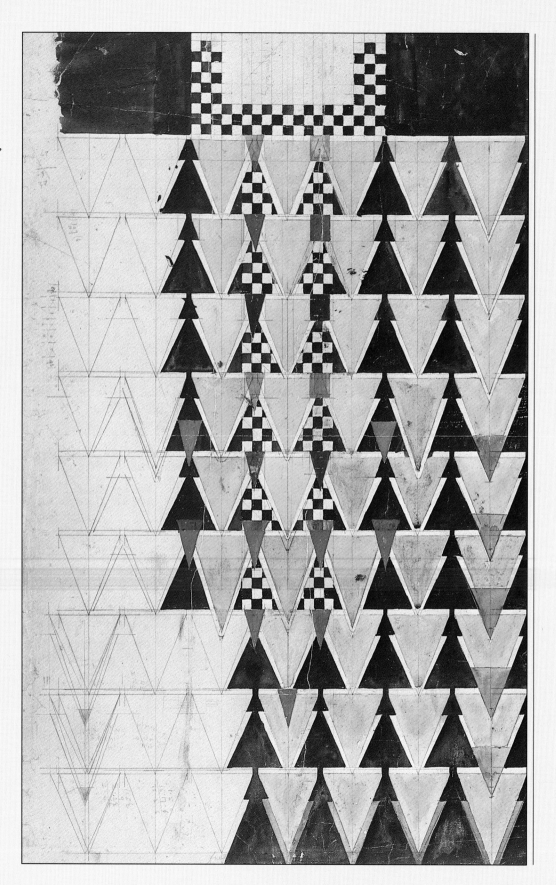

LEFT Entrance Hall fireplace, 78 Derngate, Northampton, 1916. The large fireplace designed for Bassett-Lowke's House in Northampton bears a striking resemblance to the western doorway of the Glasgow School of Art, designed some nine years earlier.

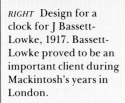

RIGHT Design for a clock for J Bassett-Lowke, 1917. Bassett-Lowke proved to be an important client during Mackintosh's years in London.

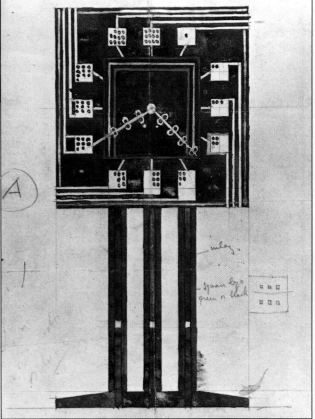

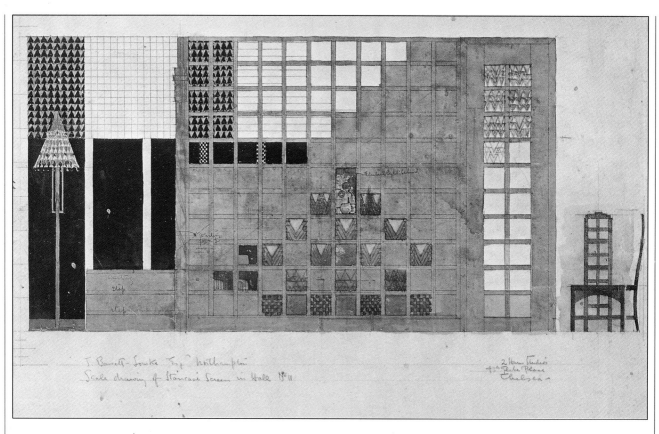

ABOVE Design for the Hall screen, 78 Derngate, Northampton (1916). A timber screen inset with small decorative panels separated the staircase from the hall.

reason to suppose that Mackintosh drank any more excessively than others. It was certainly clear that he was suffering under increasing stress, with which he was unable to cope. There were many reasons for this. It was in part due to his own personality – Mackintosh was a man of strong opinions and high idealism, and like many artists he was capable of long periods of intense activity, which proved extremely draining. At the same time he was equally prone to bouts of deep depression. He felt himself to be isolated, at the mercy of ignorant officialdom and without the help and support of his peers.

The year following his resignation the Mackintoshes closed their Glasgow home and moved to the village of Walberswick on the Suffolk coast, where there was a small artists' colony which had been frequented by the Newberys. The intention was to find peace and seclusion, an atmosphere in which Charles could recover his self-confidence. Husband and wife devoted themselves to watercolour painting, Mackintosh producing some of the finest flower studies of his career. These were supposedly in preparation for a book to be published in Germany; the outbreak of war in August 1914,

however, prevented these plans.

As soon as war was declared every stranger became an object of suspicion. The Mackintoshes, who spoke with, what seemed to the locals, foreign accents, and whose habit it was to work all day in a tiny studio and then to walk extensively about the countryside in the evening, soon became the subject of conjecture. On returning one evening, the artists found a soldier guarding their lodgings; all their papers had been examined and some correspondence with the Viennese Secessionists discovered. Mackintosh was summoned to appear before a local tribunal and it was only with great difficulty that he managed to convince magistrates that he was not a spy. It was necessary for Patrick Geddes of Edinburgh to send his daughter, later Lady Norah Mears, to the War Office to assert Mackintosh's innocence. Charles was extremely upset by the whole incident and had to be restrained from taking the matter further.

In 1915 Margaret and Charles moved to London, settling in Glebe Place, Chelsea, and renting two small adjacent studios. For a time they were very happy; Mackintosh's health was greatly improved and they found in Chelsea, particularly at The Blue Cockatoo, a nearby restaurant noted as an artists' haunt, the warmth and companionship they needed. They made many friends, several of whom subsequently became artists of international repute: Randolph Schwabe, Augustus John and, from Glasgow, Celtic Ballet-founder Margaret Morris, her husband, painter JD Fergusson, Allan Walton and James Stewart Hill.

Due to the exigencies of the war, however, architectural work was impossible to find and, of course, the Mackintoshes' work was practically unknown in London. Fortunately, Mackintosh was introduced to WJ Bassett-Lowke, the proprietor of the well-known engineering and model-making firm of that name. He commissioned from Mackintosh a number of pieces of furniture, some small graphic works and alterations to two houses. The most important project, dating to 1916, was the alteration, redecoration and furnishing of a small terraced house at 78 Derngate, Northampton, for Bassett-Lowke and his new bride.

The red-brick, Victorian house, with its front door opening directly onto the pavement, and long narrow garden at the back, presented a complete contrast to the open sites of Hill House and Windyhill. Few structural alterations were made; an extension was built at the back, increasing the interior and providing attractive balconies in the back bedrooms; the staircase was turned at right angles, producing an enlarged lounge-hall, and the parlour window was widened to 6 ft (1.8 m) and projected out to form a bay. The rear exterior of the building, with its functional simplicity, emphasis on form and proportion, and use of an enclosed balcony, seems to present the characteristics of the Modern Movement in England at an extremely early date.

The interiors of Derngate again exemplify Mackintosh's startling originality. From the decorative point of view the dramatic lounge-hall and the guest room were the most interesting areas. The hall contained a large fireplace which Mackintosh remodelled in a manner reminiscent of the west doorway of the Glasgow School of Art. The staircase was separated from the hall by a timber screen composed of open and closed squares. The walls and ceiling were painted a soft black, while the furniture and woodwork were stained black and wax-polished. The walls were divided into narrow vertical

LEFT Entrance Hall and screen, 78 Derngate, Northampton (1916). A dramatic scheme was devised for the hall of black panelling and lacquered furniture offset with triangular stencilled decoration in glowing colours and black and white chequered detailing on the walls and the carpet.

panels by a stencilled band with a white and black chequerboard pattern. The decorative frieze around the walls consisted of small, triangular stencilled motifs outlined in silver-grey and coloured golden-yellow, vermilion, blue, emerald green and purple, thus producing a rich, glowing effect throughout the room. The geometric theme was completed by the black-and-white checked carpet. Mackintosh claims that the use of black on the walls and ceiling was intended to produce a sense of mystery and spaciousness.

The guest room on the second floor (redesigned in 1919) is one of Mackintosh's most arresting interiors. The ceiling, walls and woodwork were painted white, and there was a plain grey carpet on the floor. The furniture was decorated with narrow bands of black stencilled with ultramarine squares. The twin beds were plain and simple, their only decoration consisting of six square piercings in the top rail and a checked border. The black and white stripe of the bedspreads was picked up on the wall and ceiling by a patterned paper which served to suggest a canopy linking the two beds. This was edged with ultramarine harness braid, secured

by black-headed drawing pins. Sadly, these
interiors were not illustrated in the press until
1920, and even then the designer's name was
omitted; the project did not lead on to any other
commission of importance.

The following years in Chelsea, between
1916 and 1919, were devoted to a number of
projects. The Mackintoshes became involved
with the London Salon of the Independents,
which sponsored 'open' exhibitions, and The
Plough, a theatrical society for which they
designed sets and costumes. In 1920 several
architectural projects emerged, largely through
friends and acquaintances. In January Mackintosh was asked to design a studio house on a site
in Glebe Place, Chelsea, for the painter Harold
Squire and a few weeks later, to prepare similar
schemes for Derwent Wood and A Blunt. Then
in March 1920, Mackintosh began work on a
project for a block of studio flats for the Arts
League of Service and in June on a small
theatre for Margaret Morris.

The commission for Harold Squire originally
consisted of two studios, the largest being 32 ft
by 22 ft (9.75 m by 6.7 m) and passing through
two storeys, with bedrooms behind. Mackintosh

had to modify the scheme severely due to the
client's limited funds (a cost of £6,000 was
eventually agreed on). The artist was well satisfied with the result, claiming that it was the
most magnificent studio in London. Despite his
enthusiasm, Squire occupied the building for
no more than two years: the site had originally
formed part of the large garden of a Dr Phené,
who was rumoured to have indulged in mystic
rites of an unpleasant kind. Shortly after taking
up residence in the studio, Squire heard from
the servants that they had seen the spectre of a
man on horseback and that the house was
haunted. When Squire himself saw the appari-
tion in broad daylight a medium was called in.
Apparently, the late Dr Phené had been fanati-
cally attached to a horse which had once saved
his life; the beast was buried beneath the plot
chosen for the studio and had been exhumed
during the preparation of the building site. The
ghostly visitor, which made it difficult for
Squire to find – and then keep – servants,
coupled with high maintenance costs on the
flat, led to the artist's premature move.

The studio flats for the Arts League were
intended to provide workspace and accommo-

LEFT Guestroom furniture (reconstructed room setting from 78 Derngate, Northampton). Black, white and ultramarine in the guest bedroom were used to great effect, creating a stunningly original interior.

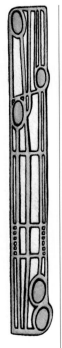

ABOVE *La Rue du Soleil, Port Vendres*, 1927. Watercolour.

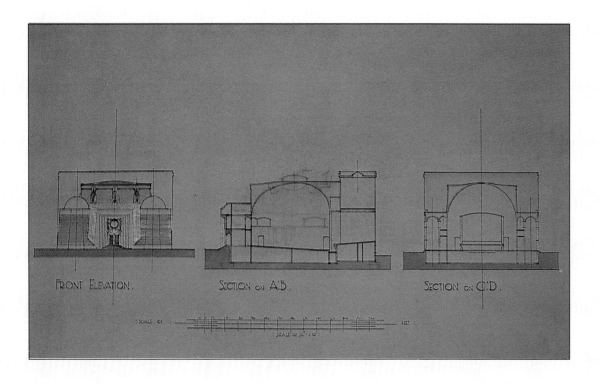

FRONT ELEVATION.   SECTION ON A:B.   SECTION ON C:D.

dation at a reasonable price, each artist-tenant being a shareholder in the property cooperative. Mackintosh's design proved unpopular with the authorities, however; among other things, they claimed that it was 'not architectural enough'. Despite the scheme eventually being passed, the building never materialized, perhaps due to lack of funds. A similar fate befell Mackintosh's last major building project, the theatre for Margaret Morris. The plans and elevations show us a formal, symmetrical structure, with an air of monumentality closer to the works of Mackintosh's Secessionist friends than to his own earlier Glasgow buildings. This was the last project of note which the architect worked on, and it affords a tantalizing glimpse of what might have been. Mackintosh's work had become, if anything, more powerful and certainly less pretty; it is hardly surprising, yet deeply dispiriting, that the conservative local authorities put a stop to such schemes.

Frustrated and disappointed, Mackintosh became morose and apathetic. On the advice of

their friends, the Mackintoshes decided to take a long holiday abroad. They settled at Port Vendres, on the Mediterranean side of the Franco-Spanish border. For four years Mackintosh devoted himself entirely to watercolour painting. He set himself the task of perfecting his technique and establishing himself as a painter. His watercolours were extraordinary; they were quite different from anything he had previously produced in the medium, possessing a strength and vigour akin to his first decorative experiments as a young man.

These paintings fell into two main categories: still lifes, which usually consisted of flowers, and landscapes. The flower paintings were exuberant and full of colour and life, but it was in the landscapes that Mackintosh most forcefully expressed himself as an architect-painter. His concern was not so much to record the natural scene before him, but rather to use shape, colour, tone and line to recreate his own vision – which was above all architectural. He was never really concerned with representing

ABOVE Design for a proposed theatre for Margaret Morris, 1920. Elevation and two sections. The symmetrical treatment resembles Vienna Successionist designs of the same period.

115

LEFT AND ABOVE *Pinks*,
watercolour.
Mackintosh's flower
paintings were
exuberant and full of
colour and life.

ABOVE *Le Fort Maillert*, 1927. Watercolour.

space and distance, and as a consequence his paintings tend to emphasize the two-dimensional reality of the picture plane. The specific architectonic quality was developed in the massing of planes and the deliberate way in which elements were built up, for example, *Le Fort Maillert* (1927), wherein the emphasis is focused on the single, dominant feature, the mass of rocks. The forms and linear patterns themselves often bear a marked resemblance to his later architectural drawings, but there is an added brilliance of colour. In *The Little Bay, Port Vendres*, also of 1927, the power of the clear, azure blue of the sky and the deeper turquoise of the sea is emphasized by the complete calm, the utter serenity, pervading the rest of the picture. Mackintosh was not interested in portraying movement or atmospheric effect. These paintings, with their emphasis on mass, form, pattern and line, are magnificent examples of architectural and decorative design – for Mackintosh painting was another dimension of architecture, the one influencing the other.

Mackintosh worked intensively; it would often take two or three weeks to finish a painting, although some were completed in a few days. He always painted in the open air and on a sunny day, refusing to work in bad weather. Margaret arranged for an exhibition at the Leicester Galleries in London, and this gave him a goal to work towards; however, Mackintosh was not pleased with the prices offered, the highest being £30.

In the autumn of 1927 Mackintosh complained of a sore throat and on medical advice returned to London, where he was diagnosed to be suffering from cancer of the tongue and throat. Despite radium treatment and a long convalescence in London he died, aged 60, on 19 December, 1928. Margaret did not survive her husband long; four years later, on 10 January, 1933, she died alone in London.

Among a small collection of letters relating to the disposition of the Mackintoshes' effects after Margaret's death, there is a terse and officious letter from a firm of London valuers, listing the contents of the Chelsea studios. A large collection of sketches and architectural drawings and 31 paintings were stated to be 'practically of no value', and the sum of £88 16s 2d was put on the total. Incredibly, a nominal value of £1 was given for four chairs of Mackintosh's own design.

ABOVE *The Village of La Lagonne,* watercolour. In 1923 the
Mackintoshes left Chelsea and settled in southern France where
for the next four years Charles devoted himself entirely to
watercolour painting.

ABOVE *The Little Bay, Port Vendres*, 1927. Watercolour.

chapter eight

EPILOGUE

Despite the efforts of a small band of enthusiasts seeking to establish Charles Rennie Mackintosh's place in history, it was in fact the sale of a single chair which made Mackintosh a household name. In 1973 a chair was bought at auction by an American collector for £9,300; the subsequent publicity attracted the attention of dealers and public alike. In the same year the Milanese firm, Cassina, began to reproduce Mackintosh furniture and the Charles Rennie Mackintosh Society was founded. With the increasing popular appeal of his work, Mackintosh has since become something of a cult figure, with firms in Spain and Canada joining Italy in making good-quality reproductions available to an international market.

Mackintosh first came to public attention in the 1950s as one of the 'pioneers' of the Modern Movement in architecture. He was widely admired for those features in his work that seemed to predict the avant-garde developments of the next generation. Seen from the perspective of the present day, when Modernism has been overtaken by Post-Modernism – in which traditional elements are combined with modern materials and dramatic colour arrangements – other aspects of his work prove just as relevant. For example, the symbolic content and reference to traditional Scottish forms which recur in Mackintosh's domestic architecture and notebooks, and the romantic concept of the studio residences in Chelsea, prove particularly stimulating in the light of a new vernacular revival.

With the renewed interest in Mackintosh, much of his work, which heretofore was sadly neglected, has been restored and made available to the public. In the late 1940s collections were formed at the Glasgow School of Art and the Hunterian Art Gallery of the University of Glasgow. As well as the original furniture and

fittings still in use in the Art School today, an important collection of architectural drawings, watercolours and furniture is displayed in the Mackintosh Room (the old Board Room) and the Furniture Gallery of the School. The Ingram Street Tea Rooms, preserved since 1950 and finally dismantled in 1971, were purchased by the Glasgow City Art Gallery and Museum at Kelvingrove, where a reconstructed section of the Chinese Room is now on view. Meanwhile, an appropriate home for the Charles Rennie Mackintosh Society was found at Queen's Cross Church, Maryhill, Glasgow, in the late 1970s.

During recent years, Hill House has passed into the hands of the National Trust for Scotland

ABOVE Panel of lettering by CR Mackintosh, 1901.

121

and is currently undergoing repairs and restoration. One wing is available to let, while the rest is open to the public. After more than half a century the Willow Tea Rooms, carelessly remodelled by the department store which had last occupied it, underwent a remarkable reversion. The reinstatement of walls, floors and windows, and the uncovering and extensive restoration and reproduction of the fittings, have effectively helped to recapture at least some of the appearance and atmosphere of the original tea-rooms.

The incorporation of the Southpark Avenue interiors in the Hunterian Art Gallery is another example of an attempt at accurate reconstruction. It represents the final stage in a prolonged effort to provide a suitable environment for the University of Glasgow's collection of the architect's work. To avoid the risk of subsidence and plans for redevelopment in that area, Mackintosh's home had been demolished in 1963, the panelling, fixtures and fittings put into storage

ABOVE Exterior of 'The Mackintosh House' (Hunterian Art Gallery) incorporating the front door and a window from Mackintosh's house at 78 Southpark Avenue.

LEFT The Mackintosh Room in the Glasgow School of Art. An important collection of Mackintosh furniture, drawings and paintings is on permanent exhibition in what used to be the Board Room. The light fittings originally hung in a private house, Windyhill, at Kilmalcolm, designed by Mackintosh *c*1899.

ABOVE House of an Art Lover (*Haus eines Kunstfreundes*), view from the south-east (1901). Almost 90 years after the designs won a special prize in a competition promoted by the German magazine *Zeitschrift für Innendekoration*, Graham Roxburgh, a long-standing Mackintosh enthusiast, plans to construct the House of an Art Lover using the surviving set of lithographs as reference, with the main interiors open to the public at weekends and on holidays.

and used later to recreate as much of the original fabric as possible. Once a special extension to the gallery was designed, the principal interiors were convincingly integrated on three floors, along with several other exhibition spaces including the Mackintosh Gallery, for the changing display of drawings and designs and a room to house a reconstruction of the guest bedroom from Derngate.

It is now possible, therefore, to see at first hand a representative range of Mackintosh buildings and interiors in a way that was not possible a few years ago. Even now there are plans under way to construct the 'Haus eines Kunstfreundes' in Glasgow. Using Mackintosh's original drawings, the intention is to create exact replicas of the building and its principal interiors, which would then be opened to the public. With 60 per cent of the estimated £1.2 million cost already pledged, it is further proof of the growing respect Mackintosh's work now commands.

The Charles Rennie Mackintosh Society is based in Queen's Cross Church (870 Garscube Road, Glasgow G20 7EL) where exhibitions, meetings and lectures are held. There is a small library and a shop selling reproductions of Charles Rennie Mackintosh's pictures and graphic work. The Society also publishes a newsletter, provides information about and access to Charles Rennie Mackintosh's buildings, and sponsors tours and events.

LEFT The Willow Tea Rooms, Glasgow. The 1979–80 restoration has helped to recapture some of the original appearance and atmosphere of the Tea Rooms.

INDEX

Page numbers in *italic* refer to the illustrations and captions

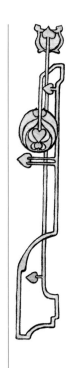

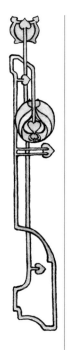

PICTURE CREDITS